MANCHESTER UNITED

–

Moments to Remember

John Creighton

First published in 1991 by Sigma Leisure – an imprint of **Sigma Press**, 1 South Oak Lane, Wilmslow, Cheshire SK9 6AR, England.

Whilst every effort has been made to ensure that the information given in this book is correct, neither the publisher nor the author accept any responsibility for any inaccuracy.

British Library Cataloguing in Publication Data
A CIP record for this book is available from the British Library.

ISBN: 1-85058-259-9

Cover and title pages design by
Design House, Marple Bridge

Typesetting and graphics by
Sigma Hi-Tech Services Ltd, Wilmslow

Printed and bound by Manchester Free Press, Paragon Mill, Jersey Street, M4 6FP. Tel: 061-236 8822.

Cover:
Bryan Robson proudly holds the European Cup Winners' Cup in 1991.

Acknowledgments
The author and publisher are grateful to Manchester United Football Club for permission to use the club crest and the cover photograph and for their help during preparation of this book. Manchester United are not responsible for any statistical or historical errors or omissions.

Thanks are extended to the Football League and to the Football Association for allowing the author to use various results, and tables. The author is grateful to the Football League for allowing him to examine archives and records at their Headquarters.

The following have been most helpful in the provision of photographic materials:
Eastern Counties Newspapers; Stoke Evening Sentinel; Bolton Evening News; Manchester Evening News; Daily Mail [Solo (p.80)]; Manchester Public Libraries; Documentary Photography Archive; W. Craven; Mr Montgomery; B. Robinson; O. Taylor. The author and publisher have done their utmost to seek permission for use of materials. If there is any more information available, we shall be pleased to reproduce it at a later date.

CONTENTS

This Season Ticket for 1890/1 admitted one person to the Newton Heath L. Y. R. Football Club. Members were asked to, "Maintain good order and conduct" on the terraces.

NEWTON HEATH (L. & Y. R.) C. & F. C.

SEASON 1890-91.

✥ Member's Ticket. ✥

Mr. _____

SEC.'s SIG.

N.B.—The Members are earnestly requested to assist the Committee as much as possible to maintain good order and conduct of the spectators while on the ground.

Half Season Closes October 31st, 1890.
Full Season Closes April 30th, 1891.

Samuel Blomeley, Printer, Blue Boar Court, Manchester,

"The Heathens"

How did the Manchester United story start?

We have to go back to the year 1878 to the Lancashire and Yorkshire Railway Company (L. Y. R.) Yard in Newton Heath, Manchester. Founded by employees of the company, the Newton Heath L. Y. R. team (nicknamed "The Heathens"), played on spare land in the North Road district of the Manchester suburb.

Because players worked during the day, games had to take place in the evenings and on Saturday afternoons, with an area of the "Three Crowns" pub serving as a changing room.

There was no red and white strip in the late 1800s as the "Heathens" turned out in green and gold shirts. No famous manager either, just the work's Superintendent. But employees quickly proved to be formidable opposition for other railway teams, and soon they were challenging clubs such as Bootle Reserves and Bolton Wanderers.

Turning Professional

1885 was an important year in this era when Newton Heath L.Y.R. became a professional club. Imagine what an effect this had on locals in the "Three Crowns", on team members, and of course on residents in the Monsall Road and North Road districts of Manchester.

The new-found professional status seemed to pay dividends, with the club winning four Manchester Cup Finals between 1885 and 1891, finishing runners-up on three other occasions.

Newton Heath L.Y.R were admitted to the Football Alliance during 1889.The alliance was later to become the Second Division. This period also saw new players moving to the Manchester Club, including full back Jack Powell, one of several Welshmen who travelled north. Making his début in 1886 the six footer had a profound influence on the team, acting as captain when they played in the Combination. The Football Combination was formed in 1888 by clubs who were unable to gain access to the Football League, and it finished in 1889.

Other important acquisitions included brothers Roger and Jack Doughty, both of whom played for Wales. When representing Newton Heath L.Y.R., Roger's inside right position allowed him to feed passes to his centre forward brother. The team finished in 8th position during the 1889/90 season, having taken on clubs as far afield as Sunderland, Grimsby and Nottingham.

By now, the Manchester Club's aspirations were increasing, with players and management displaying an air of confidence. This was demonstrated by efforts to join the Football League during 1889 and 1891, both attempts proving fruitless. However, all was not doom and gloom, with the "Heathens" finishing runners-up to Nottingham Forest in the 1891/2 Football Alliance Season.

By this time, the Football League had been enlarged to two divisions, the Second Division comprising mainly Alliance clubs. Since The Heathens and Nottingham Forest occupied the top two slots in the Alliance, they were allowed to enter Division One.

The club's first game in the top Division was against Blackburn Rovers, culminating in a 3-4 defeat for the Manchester squad. The players were Warner; Clements; Brown; Perring; Erentz; Stewart; Coupar; Farman; Donaldson; Carson; Mathieson. By now, of course, the letters L.Y.R. had been dropped from the Club's title.

First League Match Victory

October 15th 1892 was an important date for Newton Heath who won a League match for the first time. What a game! The Manchester team scored a magnificent 10 goals against Wolverhampton Wanderer's single goal. Stewart and Donaldson both had hat tricks, with other contributions coming from Hood, Hendry, Farman and Carson. The fans were certainly pleased with this victory – the first after the initial six matches in Division One.

It is the 1892/3 season, the first time Newton Heath have experienced the Football League. Finishing 16th in the table, the club had attracted reasonable crowds in this period, with 15,000 people for example, witnessing a 5–0 defeat by Sunderland in March 1893.

F.A. CUP WINNERS 1872 – 1948

Venues

1872 and 1874–92...	Kennington Oval	1895–1914..............	Crystal Palace
1873......................	Lillie Bridge	1915......................	Old Trafford, Manchester
1893......................	Fallowfield, Manchester	1920–1922..............	Stamford Bridge
1894......................	Everton	1923 to date............	Wembley

Year	Winners	Opponents	Score
1872....	Wanderers	Royal Engineers	1–0
1873....	Wanderers	Oxford University	2–0
1874....	Oxford University	Royal Engineers	2–0
1875....	Royal Engineers	Old Etonians	2–0 after drawn game
1876....	Wanderers	Old Etonians	3–0 after drawn game
1877....	Wanderers	Oxford University	2–0 after extra half hour
1878....	*Wanderers	Royal Engineers	3–1
1879....	Old Etonians	Clapham Rovers	1–0
1880....	Clapham Rovers	Oxford University	1–0
1881....	Old Carthusians	Old Etonians	3–0
1882....	Old Etonians	Blackburn Rovers	1–0
1883....	Blackburn Olympic	Old Etonians	2–1 after extra half hour
1884....	Blackburn Rovers	Queen's Park, Glasgow	2–1
1885....	Blackburn Rovers	Queen's Park, Glasgow	2–0
1886....	†Blackburn Rovers	West Bromwich Albion	2–0 after drawn game
1887....	Aston Villa	West Bromwich Albion	2–0
1888....	West Bromwich Albion	Preston North End	2–1
1889....	Preston North End	Wolverhampton Wanderers	3–0
1890....	Blackburn Rovers	Sheffield Wednesday	6–1
1891....	Blackburn Rovers	Notts County	3–1
1892....	West Bromwich Albion	Aston Villa	3–0
1893....	Wolverhampton Wanderers	Everton	1–0
1894....	Notts County	Bolton Wanderers	4–1
1895....	Aston Villa	West Bromwich Albion	1–0
1896....	Sheffield Wednesday	Wolverhampton Wanderers	2–1
1897....	Aston Villa	Everton	3–2
1898....	Nottingham Forest	Derby County	3–1
1899....	Sheffield United	Derby County	4–1
1900....	Bury	Southhampton	4–0
1901....	Tottenham Hotspur	Sheffield United	3–1 after drawn game
1902....	Sheffield United	Southhampton	2–1 after drawn game
1903....	Bury	Derby County	6–0
1904....	Manchester City	Bolton Wanderers	1–0
1905....	Aston Villa	Newcastle United	2–0
1906....	Everton	Newcastle United	1–0
1907....	Sheffield Wednesday	Everton	2–1
1908....	Wolverhampton Wanderers	Newcastle United	3–1
1909....	Manchester United	Bristol City	1–0
1910....	Newcastle United	Barnsley	2–0 after drawn game
1911....	Bradford City	Newcastle United	1–0 after drawn game
1912....	Barnsley	West Bromwich Albion	1–0 after drawn game
1913....	Aston Villa	Sunderland	1–0
1914....	Burnley	Liverpool	1–0
1915....	Sheffield United	Chelsea	3–0
1920....	Aston Villa	Huddersfield Town	1–0 after extra time
1921....	Tottenham Hotspur	Wolverhampton Wanderers	1–0
1922....	Huddersfield Town	Preston North End	1–0
1923....	Bolton Wanderers	West Ham United	2–0
1924....	Newcastle United	Aston Villa	2–0
1925....	Sheffield United	Cardiff City	1–0
1926....	Bolton Wanderers	Manchester City	1–0
1927....	Cardiff City	Arsenal	1–0
1928....	Blackburn Rovers	Huddersfield Town	3–1
1929....	Bolton Wanderers	Portsmouth	2–0
1930....	Arsenal	Huddersfield Town	2–0
1931....	West Bromwich Albion	Birmingham	2–1
1932....	Newcastle United	Arsenal	2–1
1933....	Everton	Manchester City	3–0
1934....	Manchester City	Portsmouth	2–1
1935....	Sheffield Wednesday	West Bromwich Albion	4–2
1936....	Arsenal	Sheffield United	1–0
1937....	Sunderland	Preston North End	3–1
1938....	Preston North End	Huddersfield Town	1–0 after extra time
1939....	Portsmouth	Wolverhampton Wanderers	4–1
1946....	Derby County	Charlton Athletic	4–1
1947....	Charlton Athletic	Burnley	1–0
1948....	Manchester United	Blackpool	4–2

* Won outright, but restored to the Association.
† A special trophy was awarded for third consecutive win.

Test Matches and Division Two

A real crowd-puller of the early 1890s was the so-called 'Test Match' played between the top three clubs of Division Two and the bottom three of Division One, the results deciding the promotions and relegations.

A crucial tie occurred on April 22nd 1893 involving Newton Heath and Second Division champions, Small Heath (later to become Birmingham City). A crowd of 4,000 witnessed a 1-1 draw, necessitating a replay at Sheffield the following week. This resulted in a 5-2 victory for the Manchester club, thus guaranteeing another season in the First Division.

The Club was trying to develop a more professional image, which led to the acquisition of a new ground. The team moved from North Street to Bank Street, Clayton, which was overshadowed by a chemical works and factories. Although the first game against Burnley resulted in a 3-2 win, the omens were not good. In fact, during the 1893/4 season, the "Heathens" won only six games out of a total of 30 Division One matches, and the close of the 1893/4 season found the Club wallowing at the foot of the First Division, having lost 22 of their 30 games.

Once more the test matches were on the horizon, and in the all important deciding game, Liverpool's victory of 2-0 sent Newton Heath into Division Two. There was some consolation, however, in 1894 when the Club reached the second round of the FA Cup.

Manchester City "Derby" games

The rivalry between Manchester City and Manchester United really comes to a head each year when the Clubs face each other – a game at Maine Road, then one at Old Trafford. These "Derby" matches are often seen as the highlights of Manchester's football calendar and can be traced back to 1894. Both Division Two clubs had their first confrontation at City's ground which was then located on Hyde Road. The outcome of this memorable match was a resounding 5-2 win for Newton Heath with four goals by Smith and one from Clarkin. The return game later on in the season resulted in a 4-1 victory for the "Heathens".

Two years later, in 1896, the club's colours were changed to white shirts and blue shorts, taking them into the next century.

MANCHESTER UNITED FOOTBALL CLUB

1900s

United - the new name

The St Bernard Dog

1902 was a crucial year financially, as talk of bankruptcy worried the Newton Heath management and of course, the supporters. Help came from a surprising quarter.

In order to raise much needed cash, a fête was held at St. James' Hall, Manchester, at which a St. Bernard dog was led amongst the crowd by team captain Harry Stafford. The idea was for people to place money in a collecting box around the animal's neck.

Fortunately (or unfortunately) the dog wandered off and was subsequently adopted by Mr. Davies, a local brewer. Eventually, Harry Stafford traced his animal to the businessman and, naturally, the story of the club's financial plight was recounted by the Newton Heath player. Mr. Davies offered to help, thus saving the club from financial embarrassment.

The sequel to this is yet another milestone in the United saga, since the benefactor became Chairman of Newton Heath in 1902.

New Name, New People

In April 1902, the name MANCHESTER UNITED first appeared, following discussions on a new title – with other suggestions being Manchester Celtic or Manchester Central. Around this time, the famous red shirt and white shorts became the club's official strip.

The first game as the "Reds" took place in September 1902 when United defeated Gainsborough Trinity. It must have been quite an occasion for the supporters to read the score in their local paper:

| Manchester United | 1 |
| Gainsborough Trinity | 0 |

There were eighteen clubs in the 1902/3 Second Division. The top teams may hold something of interest for City fans:

Position	Team	Points
1	Manchester City	54
2	Small Heath	51
3	Woolwich Arsenal	48
4	Bristol City	42
5	Manchester United	38

By now, United attracted a considerable following, as shown by some 25,000 people who attended a League game against Small Heath in November 1902.

The following year was noteworthy in terms of new personnel joining United. The great Ernest Mangnall was appointed secretary/manager, and quickly became a dynamic figure within the Club, buying crowd-pullers like Alex Bell, Charlie Roberts and Robert Bonthron. This last player was a hardy Scot, and Bell teamed up with other half back stalwarts such as Dick Duckworth and Charlie Roberts, the latter having been signed for a £450 fee.

At the close of the 1904/5 season, United were positioned third in Division Two, and they had played Fulham three times in the FA Cup. The Londoners defeated the Reds 1-0 in a second FA Cup replay game at Villa Park, on 23rd January 1905.

Mangnall's effect on United was demonstrated in the 1905/6 season when the club finished runners-up behind Bristol City, thus securing promotion to Division One. This was a happy time for the loyal fans who had given their unstinting support for 12 years of Second Division soccer. In the 1905/6 FA Cup competition, United had beaten Staple Hill, Norwich City and Aston Villa before meeting Woolwich Arsenal in Round Four. This tie on March 10th 1906 saw the London Club win 3-2, with goals for the Reds scored by Peddie and Sagar.

The victorious United team have just arrived at Central Station, from where they travel by horse-drawn carriage to Manchester Town Hall. Jubilant fans thronged the streets to welcome the team who defeated Bristol 1–0 in the FA Cup Final, when A. Turnbull supplied the winning goal in April 1909.

The United squad for the 1911/12 season contained several household names, including Meredith, Duckworth, Roberts and Turnbull. These players are on the first four seats on the middle row, (left to right).

Manchester United FC, 1913-14.
Back row (l to r) Hodge, Gripps, Knowles, Beale,
Stacey, Hamill, Whalley.
Front row (l to r) Meredith, Woodcock, Anderson,
West, Wall.

It was in the 1906/7 season that rivals Manchester City and United were both playing in the First Division. The results of the two memorable meetings were –

Date	Result	Comments
Dec 1 1906	City won 3–0	Away match for United in front of 40,000 spectators
April 6 1907	Draw 1-1	Home game for United with a goal by Roberts

Meredith

If one had to single out a player who caused a stir amongst Manchester soccer fans around this period, it would be Billy Meredith, a flamboyant player who was the football supporter's delight.

His transfer to United from City in the 1906/7 season caused consternation among the City ranks, especially because fellow City players Sandy Turnbull, Burgess and Bannister also moved over to the Reds. This followed allegations that Meredith had attempted to bribe an Aston Villa player to enable City to win the game. Seventeen City players, who were judged to have received illegal payments, were barred from playing for their club again. This allowed Mangnall to secure the City players so easily.

Billy remained with United until 1921, making 332 appearances and scoring 35 goals in League and FA Cup matches.. In 1908, United celebrated their first League championship, taking 52 points from 38 games, and were 9 points ahead of runners-up Aston Villa.

First Cup Final

April 24th 1909 features prominently in club records – the day when Manchester United reached their first FA Cup Final, meeting Bristol City at Crystal Palace, London.

The route to this match saw victories over Brighton and Hove Albion, Everton, Blackburn Rovers and Burnley. The semi-final against Newcastle was held on March 27th 1909 at Bramall Lane where a Halse goal gave the Manchester club a 1-0 victory.

And so to the Final where 71,000 spectators enjoyed a dazzling display by Meredith, with Sandy Turnbull's goal clinching the 1-0 victory over Bristol City.

An enthusiastic crowd welcomed the jubilant team at Manchester's Central Station from where they made the short journey to the Town Hall. On arrival, captain Charlie Roberts showed the faithful the FA Cup.

As a point of interest, the train fare for the excursion to Crystal Palace where the Final took place, cost 11 shillings (55 pence) for a day return, or 12 shillings and sixpence if supporters left Manchester on the Friday evening.

Old Trafford and League Champions

By 1910, things were moving apace and Chairman, John Davies, was clearly impressed by United's success, donating £60,000 for the purposes of buying a site and building a stadium in Old Trafford.

Yet another milestone in the club's history! The last game to be played at the dowdy Clayton ground took place in front of 7,000 fans on January 22nd 1910, when Tottenham were trounced 5-0, as the Manchester team exploited the opponents' weaknesses with ferocity and skill.

The move to Old Trafford was in February 1910 with the first game taking place on the 19th of that month. Some 50,000 people witnessed a match where seven goals were scored, and although at one stage United were ahead 2-0, they eventually lost 4-3. The first players to score for United at their new stadium were Homer, Turnbull and Wall.

The 1910 season brought further acclaim as the club became League Champions following a tense struggle against Aston Villa who were just one point ahead of the Manchester Club. In the closing matches of the season, the Midlands team had to meet Liverpool while United were up against Sunderland. The Manchester supporters were agog with excitement in the second half of April 1911 – on the 22nd of this month, the team lost 4-2 to Aston Villa, while seven days later, the all important games were played. Aston Villa went down 3-1 to Liverpool and the Old Trafford crowd cheered on the Reds who thrashed Sunderland 5-1 on April 29th. United grasped the Division One Championship with one point in their favour. Overleaf is how the top places looked at the close of the 1910/11 season.

Manchester City were 17th with 31 points.

First Division 1910/11		
Position	Team	Points
1	Manchester United	52
2	Aston Villa	51
3	Sunderland	45
4	Everton	45
5	Bradford City	45
6	Wednesday	42

Year	Division One Leaders	United's Position
1911/12	Blackburn	13th
1912/13	Sunderland	4th
1913/14	Blackburn	14th
1914/15	Everton	18th

The two sides representing City and United in a 1914 clash. This extract from a programme shows some alterations alongside original team names, suggesting late changes just before kick-off. In the period 1913-1915, the two clubs met on four occasions, each side winning one game, the remaining two finishing in draws.

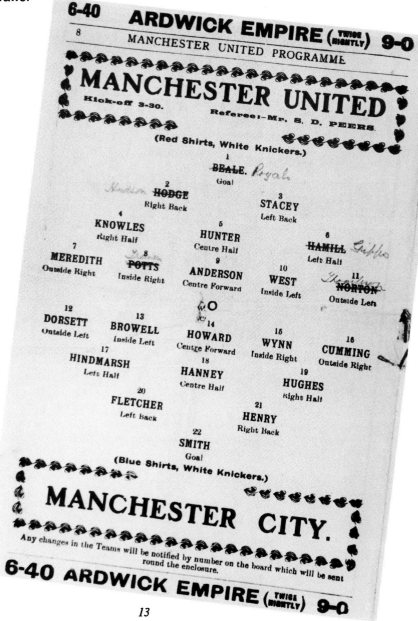

Comings and Goings

The stars of this era included such people as Meredith, Turnbull, Duckworth and Bell. An important event in the United story occurred when Ernest Mangnall decided to join rivals Manchester City. How did it affect the Reds? Just consider the records – the club did not win another League Championship for over 40 years.

There was an exodus of experienced players who sought pastures new, leaving a particular weakness in the half back line. Alex Bell transferred to Blackburn in 1913 while colleague Charlie Roberts continued his career with Oldham in the same year. Interestingly, Bell left just after World War One, to become trainer with Coventry City. He later moved back to Manchester to assume a similar rôle with City.

With war looming on the horizon, United were struggling in the League. Sadly, the war took its toll on many players including Sandy Turnbull who was killed in France.

AERIAL VIEW OF THE UNITED FOOTBALL GROUND

An aerial photograph of United's Old Trafford stadium in the 1920s, some 10 years after it was built. A few years before this photograph was taken, the 1915 FA Cup was staged at the ground, when Sheffield defeated Chelsea 3-0. This match was nicknamed the "Khaki Final" owing to the large number of servicemen in the crowd. Record receipts at Old Trafford were taken at the game against Legia Warsaw in April 1991. The second leg of the semi-final in the European Cup-Winners' Cup brought in £432,345.80.

Can this really be a bunch of Stretford-enders at Old Trafford? This 1935 half-time scene depicts a group of fans, some of whom are wearing waistcoats and ties. One wonders what the man at the front is quaffing!

Division Two Soccer – The F.A. Cup Final

Division Two soccer returned to Old Trafford in 1921/22. United's 22nd position in Division One resulting in relegation. The supporters were a bit happier when the renowned Frank Barson signed for the club in the 1922/23 season for £5,000 from Aston Villa. He stayed with the Reds until 1927/28, appearing in 140 League games and 12 FA Cup matches, frustrating many opponents with a series of brilliant performances.

Another new strip emerged during 1923 – white shorts and similar coloured shirts displaying a red 'V'.

1925/26 brought a couple of moments to savour. United bounced back into Division One, finishing a respectable 9th, and they provided fans with a series of good matches in the run up to the FA Cup Final. The club defeated Port Vale, Tottenham, Sunderland and Fulham before embarking on a memorable semi-final against Manchester City.

Held at Bramall Lane on 27th March, the game resulted in a 3-0 win for City who subsequently lost the Final to Bolton Wanderers.

This was United's Cup semi-final team of 1925/26, defeated by Manchester City at Bramall Lane. A crowd of just over 46,500 saw United go down 3–0 to their rivals.

Charlie Mitten (left), who went to Bogota after United's visit to America. Seen here with Jack Rowley – known as "The Gunner" by virtue of his powerful shooting.

Financial Problems and New Bosses

Financial problems overshadowed the club in the early 1930s, but what can be termed a great moment in the United story was the generous help provided by James W. Gibson. The Manchester businessman's donation of £22,000 allowed the club to settle debts and to acquire new players. The benefactor became club chairman, and A. Scott Duncan was appointed manager in July 1932, succeeding Herbert Bamlett.

One respected person from this era was Walter Crickmer, who, along with Louis Rocca, managed the team from 1931-32 during the period between Bamlett's departure and Scott Duncan's arrival. He carried out similar duties in the 1937-45 period until the appointment of Matt Busby as manager. Walter deserves all the credit for the Manchester United Junior Athletics Club, drawing up a list of rules and providing a gym, trainer and coach for the young players. He is perhaps best remembered as club secretary, carrying on his sterling work until his name featured among the fatalities at Munich.

Division Three Threat and New Players

If you were a United supporter in 1933/4 then you would surely consider this to be a crucial period as the great club battled to keep out of Division Three.

In the last weekend of that season, the team faced Millwall knowing that only a win would guarantee the Manchester club a place in the Second Division during the following season. On May 5th, 1934, just over 24,000 fans packed the Millwall ground to watch the match. Luckily, Cape and Manley produced a couple of goals to make it 2-0 for United, the team finishing 20th in Division Two, just one place above Millwall.

Any great club depends heavily on the calibre of its players, and there were many people who contributed to the success of the team.

A number of players acquired in the 1930s were particularly influential. The celebrated Jack Rowley, Johnny Carey and Stan Pearson were especially significant along with goalkeeper Tommy Breen and John Smith.

Breen made 65 league and 6 FA Cup appearances in the two year spell he did from 1936. Smith had 5 FA Cup games and 37 League matches in his stint with the club between 1937 and 1945.

The famous Jack Rowley joined the club from Bournemouth in October 1937 following payment of a £3,000 fee. During his 18 years at Old Trafford, Jack found the back of the net on 208 occasions, scoring 26 in those all important FA Cup games. He was a player who combined sound intelligence with devastating results.

Stan Pearson's legendary inside left skills thrilled thousands when he turned out between 1937 and 1954. From his many marvellous contributions to the United success story one superb highlight was on March 13th 1948, when United beat Derby County 3-1 in the FA Cup semi-final. The Final at Wembley brought a 4-2 victory for the Manchester team with goals from Rowley (2), Anderson and yet again Pearson.

The distinguished Johnny Carey received the FA Cup from George VI at the 1948 Final and represented United from 1937-1953, making 306 League and 38 FA Cup appearances. The Irish international's awards included an FA Cup Winner's medal, caps for both Eire and Northern Ireland plus a League Championship Medal. As numerous opposition defences discovered, there was simply no answer to Carey's runs at goal and his determined performance.

The Youth Policy and World War II

Ardent supporters of the club will appreciate how important United's youth policy has been over the years. But when did it really start? Many people would argue that its inception was in 1938 when MUJACS (Manchester United Junior Athletic Club) was launched. This contributed to the Reds winning the Central League Championship for the first time in 18 years, because the club had a large selection of younger players from which to choose.

The outbreak of hostilities saw United in 14th position of Division One at a time when Everton occupied the top spot at the close of the 1938/39 season.

Old Trafford was severely damaged by enemy bombs on the night of March 11th 1941. The main stand, offices and dressing room were all destroyed in a raid which was intended to target Trafford Park where arms and ammunition were being manufactured. Neighbours City kindly offered the Maine Road Stadium for United's League and Cup matches and the Reds played there until 1949. It must have been quite a spectacle at Maine Road as United fans cheered on their team at City's ground.

The numbers did not fall either, with some 82,000 people turning up to see a 1-1 draw with Arsenal in a 1948 League game. Moving back to a refurbished Old Trafford in August 1949, the first game resulted in a 3-0 victory over Bolton Wanderers with a side featuring Crompton, Carey, Aston, Warner, Lynn, Cockburn, Delaney, Downie, Rowley, Pearson and Mitten.

Bolton Wanderers attack United's goal at Burnden Park on August 31st, 1949. Aston and Crompton are on United's goal line in the match which was a 2-1 victory for the Reds

F.A. CUP COMPETITION 1947 – 48

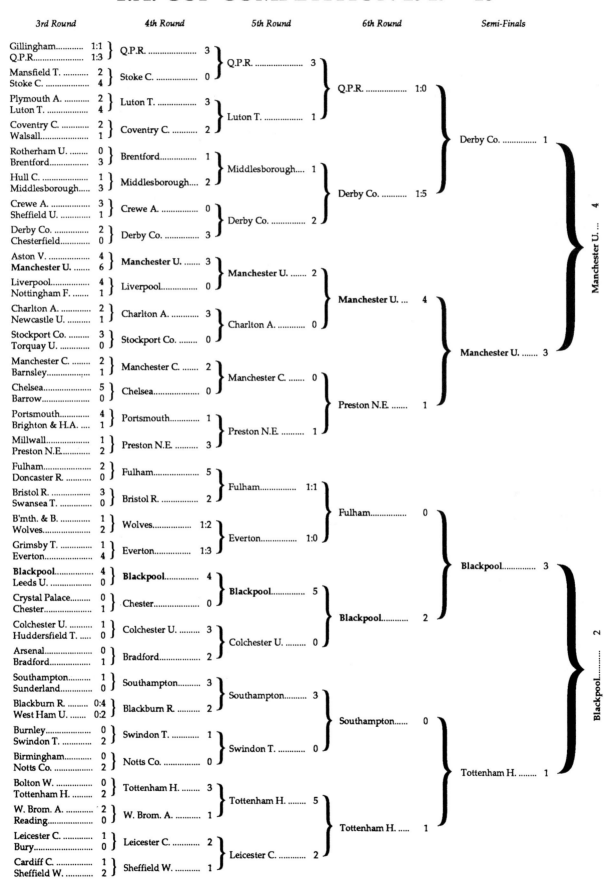

3rd Round	4th Round	5th Round	6th Round	Semi-Finals

Gillingham...... 1:1
Q.P.R....... 1:3 → Q.P.R. 3
Mansfield T. 2
Stoke C. ...... 4 → Stoke C. 0
→ Q.P.R. 3
Plymouth A. 2
Luton T. ...... 4 → Luton T. 3
Coventry C. 2
Walsall...... 1 → Coventry C. 2
→ Luton T. 1
→ Q.P.R. 1:0
Rotherham U. 0
Brentford...... 3 → Brentford...... 1
Hull C. 1
Middlesborough..... 3 → Middlesborough.... 2
→ Middlesborough.... 1
Crewe A. 3
Sheffield U. ...... 1 → Crewe A. 0
Derby Co. 2
Chesterfield...... 0 → Derby Co. 3
→ Derby Co. 2
→ Derby Co. 1:5
→ Derby Co. 1

Aston V. 4
Manchester U. ...... 6 → Manchester U. 3
Liverpool...... 4
Nottingham F. ...... 1 → Liverpool...... 0
→ Manchester U. 2
Charlton A. 2
Newcastle U. ...... 1 → Charlton A. 3
Stockport Co. 3
Torquay U. ...... 0 → Stockport Co. 0
→ Charlton A. 0
→ Manchester U. ... 4
Manchester C. 2
Barnsley...... 1 → Manchester C. 2
Chelsea...... 5
Barrow...... 0 → Chelsea...... 0
→ Manchester C. 0
Portsmouth...... 4
Brighton & H.A. .... 1 → Portsmouth...... 1
Millwall...... 1
Preston N.E. ...... 2 → Preston N.E. 3
→ Preston N.E. 1
→ Preston N.E. 1
→ Manchester U. 3

→ Manchester U. 4

Fulham...... 2
Doncaster R. ...... 0 → Fulham...... 5
Bristol R. 3
Swansea T. ...... 0 → Bristol R. 2
→ Fulham...... 1:1
B'mth. & B. 1
Wolves...... 2 → Wolves...... 1:2
Grimsby T. 1
Everton...... 4 → Everton...... 1:3
→ Everton...... 1:0
→ Fulham...... 0

Blackpool...... 4
Leeds U. ...... 0 → Blackpool...... 4
Crystal Palace...... 0
Chester...... 1 → Chester...... 0
→ Blackpool...... 5
Colchester U. 1
Huddersfield T. ...... 0 → Colchester U. 3
Arsenal...... 0
Bradford...... 1 → Bradford...... 2
→ Colchester U. 0
→ Blackpool...... 2
→ Blackpool...... 3

Southampton...... 1
Sunderland...... 0 → Southampton...... 3
Blackburn R. 0:4
West Ham U. ...... 0:2 → Blackburn R. 2
→ Southampton...... 3
Burnley...... 0
Swindon T. ...... 2 → Swindon T. 1
Birmingham...... 0
Notts Co. ...... 2 → Notts Co. 0
→ Swindon T. 0
→ Southampton...... 0
→ Tottenham H. 1

Bolton W. 0
Tottenham H. ...... 2 → Tottenham H. 3
W. Brom. A. 2
Reading...... 0 → W. Brom. A. 1
→ Tottenham H. 5
Leicester C. 1
Bury...... 0 → Leicester C. 2
Cardiff C. 1
Sheffield W. ...... 2 → Sheffield W. 1
→ Leicester C. 2
→ Tottenham H. 1

→ Blackpool...... 2

Manchester U. 4

Blackpool...... 2

When enemy bombs blitzed Old Trafford in 1941, Manchester City offered Maine Road to United for their League and Cup matches. The Reds used the ground for eight years, as shown here in April 1949 when 47,653 spectators enjoyed watching United defeat Bolton 3–0. No high fences around the pitch at this game, where Rowley scored 2 goals, with Mitten providing the other.

Busby Arrives

The 15th February 1945 should be a date never to be forgotten in the United story, since it was then that one of the most important decisions was taken by the club. The board appointed a former Scottish International half back as the new manager. Matt Busby was his name – a man who had made excellent contributions to Liverpool and Manchester City and who was captain of Scotland during the War.

Did Walter Crickmer and the board ever realise what an effect Matt Busby would have on the club? Born in 1909 in a small village not far from Glasgow, Matt left home in 1928 to play at Maine Road, moving to Liverpool during 1936. The War years saw him serving in the King's Liverpool Regiment before transferring to the Army's Physical Training Corps.

Initially, Busby was offered a three year contract by chairman James Gibson, but Matt insisted on a five year agreement which would allow him sufficient time to establish a strong team. This he did in no uncertain manner, becoming one of the first managers to actually train with the players.

Subsequent pages in this book are a testimony to the work of a man who was team manager from 1945-69 and general manager in the 1969-71 period. Matt Busby later became a United director and then president of the club.

Matt Busby's determination, leadership, vision and direction brought numerous awards to Old Trafford including the League title, European Cup and FA Cup.

Here's a question you can ask over a pint of bitter:

"Who was Matt Busby's first signing?"

The answer – Welsh international, Jimmy Murphy who served with West Bromwich before moving to United as coach in 1945. His appointment signified the start of a dynamic relationship with Matt Busby. Jimmy was coach from 1945-55, working as assistant manager from 1953-71, with a short spell as acting manager during 1958. Although Jimmy Murphy died in 1989, his contributions to Old Trafford will always be remembered.

Some Busby Signings

The club of the 1940s had a core of experienced players including Jack Rowley, Stan Pearson, Johnny Carey, John Aston, left winger Charlie Mitten and goal keeper Jack Crompton. The new manager began to use Aston and Carey as full backs instead of inside forwards. Their flair led to many constructive moves from United's rearguard which foxed numerous opposing defences. The new players were soon joined by Jimmy Delaney, signed up by Matt Busby from Celtic for £5,000.

Jimmy Delaney made important contributions to the club, staying with the Reds until his departure to Aberdeen in 1950, having played over 180 games at League and FA Cup Level. Sadly he died, like Jimmy Murphy in 1989.

So what about Matt Busby's early influence on United? The first full season after the War (1946/7) saw the club finish second in the League, just a point behind Liverpool, with the Central League title going to the reserve team.

League success is certainly part of the Reds' story, as exemplified by the first half dozen years after the Second World War. Just look at the League tables:

Year	Position	Club	Points
1946/7	1st	Liverpool	57
	2nd	Manchester United	56
1947/8	1st	Arsenal	59
	2nd	Manchester United	52
1948/9	1st	Portsmouth	58
	2nd	Manchester United	53
1949/50	1st	Portsmouth	53
	4th	Manchester United	50
1950/1	1st	Tottenham	60
	2nd	Manchester United	56
1951/2	1st	Manchester United	57
	2nd	Tottenham	53

This last season was the first time in 40 years that the Reds had won the Division One Championship title.

F.A. CUP COMPETITION 1948 – 49

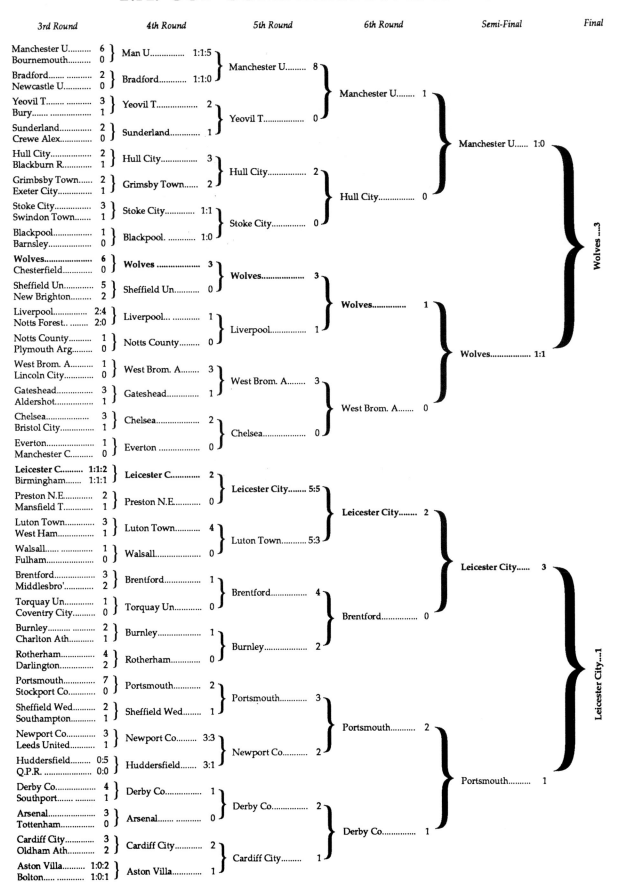

3rd Round	4th Round	5th Round	6th Round	Semi-Final	Final

Manchester U. 6
Bournemouth .... 0 } Man U. .... 1:1:5 }
Bradford 2
Newcastle U. .... 0 } Bradford .... 1:1:0 } Manchester U. .... 8 }
Yeovil T. 3
Bury .... 1 } Yeovil T. .... 2 } Yeovil T. .... 0 } Manchester U. .... 1 }
Sunderland 2
Crewe Alex .... 0 } Sunderland .... 1 }
Hull City 2
Blackburn R. .... 1 } Hull City .... 3 } Hull City .... 2 } Manchester U. ...... 1:0 }
Grimsby Town 2
Exeter City .... 1 } Grimsby Town ...... 2 } Hull City .... 0 }
Stoke City 3
Swindon Town ...... 1 } Stoke City .... 1:1 } Stoke City .... 0 }
Blackpool 1
Barnsley .... 0 } Blackpool. .... 1:0 }
Wolves 6
Chesterfield .... 0 } Wolves .... 3 } Wolves .... 3 } Wolves .... 1 } Wolves ...3
Sheffield Un. 5
New Brighton .... 2 } Sheffield Un. .... 0 }
Liverpool 2:4
Notts Forest. .... 2:0 } Liverpool... .... 1 } Liverpool .... 1 } Wolves .... 1:1 }
Notts County 1
Plymouth Arg .... 0 } Notts County .... 0 }
West Brom. A 1
Lincoln City .... 0 } West Brom. A .... 3 } West Brom. A .... 3 }
Gateshead 3
Aldershot .... 1 } Gateshead .... 1 } West Brom. A .... 0 }
Chelsea 3
Bristol City .... 1 } Chelsea .... 2 } Chelsea .... 0 }
Everton 1
Manchester C. .... 0 } Everton .... 0 }
Leicester C. 1:1:2
Birmingham .... 1:1:1 } Leicester C. .... 2 } Leicester City. .... 5:5 }
Preston N.E. 2
Mansfield T. .... 1 } Preston N.E. .... 0 } Leicester City. .... 2 }
Luton Town 3
West Ham .... 1 } Luton Town .... 4 } Luton Town .... 5:3 }
Walsall 1
Fulham .... 0 } Walsall .... 0 } Leicester City ...... 3 }
Brentford 3
Middlesbro'. .... 2 } Brentford .... 1 } Brentford .... 4 }
Torquay Un. 1
Coventry City .... 0 } Torquay Un. .... 0 } Brentford .... 0 }
Burnley 2
Charlton Ath. .... 1 } Burnley .... 1 } Burnley .... 2 }
Rotherham 4
Darlington .... 2 } Rotherham .... 0 }
Portsmouth 7
Stockport Co. .... 0 } Portsmouth .... 2 } Portsmouth .... 3 } Leicester City ...1
Sheffield Wed. 2
Southampton .... 1 } Sheffield Wed. .... 1 } Portsmouth .... 2 }
Newport Co. 3
Leeds United .... 1 } Newport Co. .... 3:3 } Newport Co. .... 2 }
Huddersfield 0:5
Q.P.R. .... 0:0 } Huddersfield .... 3:1 } Portsmouth .... 1 }
Derby Co. 4
Southport .... 1 } Derby Co. .... 1 } Derby Co. .... 2 }
Arsenal 3
Tottenham .... 0 } Arsenal .... 0 } Derby Co. .... 1 }
Cardiff City 3
Oldham Ath. .... 2 } Cardiff City .... 2 } Cardiff City .... 1 }
Aston Villa 1:0:2
Bolton .... 1:0:1 } Aston Villa .... 1 }

The "Busby Stars" who represented United between 1947 and 1951. The first memorable victory for Matt Busby occured in April 1948, when United defeated Blackpool 4–2 at Wembley in the F.A. Cup final. His squad comprised some of those pictured here:
Crompton; Carey; Aston; Anderson; Chilton; Cockburn; Delaney; Morris; Rowley; Pearson; Mitten.

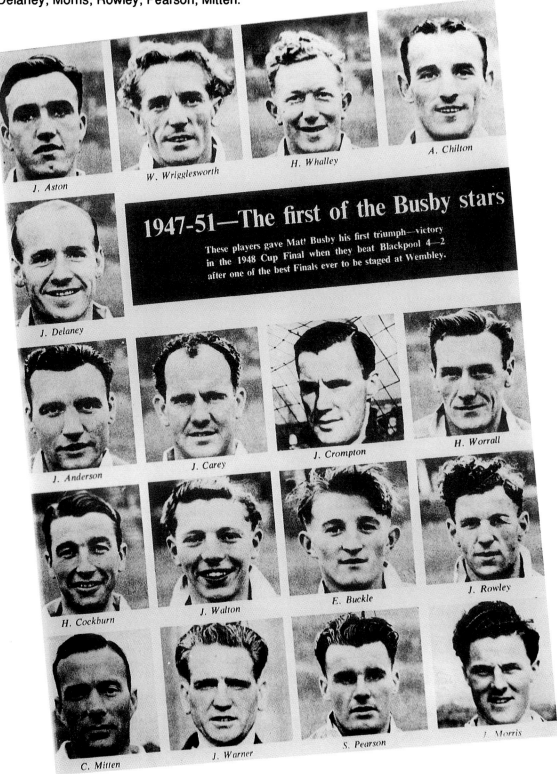

1947-51—The first of the Busby stars

These players gave Matt Busby his first triumph—victory in the 1948 Cup Final when they beat Blackpool 4—2 after one of the best Finals ever to be staged at Wembley.

J. Aston

W. Wrigglesworth

H. Whalley

A. Chilton

J. Delaney

J. Anderson

J. Carey

J. Crompton

H. Worrall

H. Cockburn

J. Walton

E. Buckle

J. Rowley

C. Mitten

J. Warner

S. Pearson

J. Morris

The 1948 FA Cup Final

The run up to this prestigious award involved several spectacular matches when United found the back of the net on 18 occasions in just 5 ties. Let's examine the road to the Cup:

January 10th 1948
Round 3 -v- Aston Villa.
Score 6-4

What a game this turned out to be – with United trailing 1-0 in the first half minute. Suddenly the team's strenuous efforts produced a complete reversal of the situation, with half time seeing United ahead by five goals to one! Villa fought back after the break, notching up 3 more goals and finally, Stan Pearson made it 6-4 for the Manchester club.

January 24th 1948
Round 4 -v- Liverpool.
Score 3-0

Played at Goodison Park in front of 74,000 people, this match saw Liverpool succumb to goals by Morris, Rowley and Mitten.

February 7th 1948
Round 5 -v- Charlton Athletic.
Score 2-0

The venue was Leeds Road, Huddersfield, where a crowd of 33,000 witnessed Warner and Mitten find the necessary couple of goals.

February 28th 1948
Round 6 -v- Preston N.E.
Score 4-1

Maine Road was the scene of this exciting game enjoyed by a large crowd at just over 74,000 who saw goals by Pearson (2), Rowley and Mitten.

March 13th 1948
Semi-final -v- Derby County.
Score 3-1

This classic semi-final took place at Hillsborough where 1946 Cup Winners Derby County were determined to pull off another victory. Those privileged to attend could argue that this memor-

able game was possibly one of the greatest of the late 1940s, with Stan Pearson providing a hat trick. These were just three of his 21 FA Cup goals during his stay with United from 1937-1954.

April 24th 1948
Cup Final -v- Blackpool.
Score 4-2

A large crowd of 99,000 attended this Wembley spectacle where English internationals Stanley Matthews and Stan Mortensen paraded on to the turf with the Blackpool squad. The second player was often referred to as the 'Blackpool Bombshell', scoring almost 200 goals in League matches for Blackpool. Matthews had moved from Stoke to Blackpool in 1947, and of course, this soccer wizard teamed up with Finney, Lawton and Mannion to form a superb England forward line.

Pundits would argue that this Cup Final was one of the finest to be played on Wembley's hallowed turf, with Blackpool ahead by a penalty at half time when the score line was 2-1. This situation lasted until 20 minutes from the 90 minute whistle, when United injected even more flair and daring into the contest with the second half bringing three dynamic goals.

Rowley headed a Morris free kick into the net in the 69th minute, this followed by a devastating shot from Pearson, which did not herald the end of the thriller. A 30 yard drive from Anderson brought the final score to 4-2, a fitting result for a game of exciting, attacking soccer. United's team was:

Crompton; Carey; Aston; Anderson; Chilton; Cockburn; Delaney; Morris; Rowley; Pearson; Mitten.

Ten thousand supporters packed the streets along the processional route from Brooklands roundabout, along Princess Road, Denmark Road then Oxford Road and into Albert Square. Outside the Town Hall, dozens of policemen and even a fire engine were employed to clear a path for the victors. Little wonder there was much jubilation – it had been 39 years since United had pulled off an FA Cup Final win, when Bristol City were defeated 1-0.

Roger Byrne, Ray Wood

New blood was brought to United in 1949. The immensely talented Roger Byrne joined the club that year, making his first League appearance in November 1951. What a player this Manchester-born young man proved to be, gaining 33 England caps and turning out over 270 times for United in League, FA Cup and European matches. Roger took over the captaincy from Johnny Carey and was a force to be reckoned with as he weaved his way down the left of the field. A tough, consistent player, he perished in the Munich disaster.

Ray Wood moved to United from Darlington in 1949 at 18 years of age. He survived the United Munich disaster and played 205 games for United. Initially back-up for Jack Crompton, Ray became the regular first team keeper in the 1954/5 season. A brilliant player, who is perhaps best remembered for his collision with Peter McParland in the 1957 Cup Final against Aston Villa. When Harry Gregg assumed regular first team goalkeeping duties, Ray Wood moved to Huddersfield Town in 1958, before joining a number of UK and overseas clubs.

The FA Cup and League 1949

During 1948/9, United met a number of formidable sides on their way to the FA Cup semi-final, including giant killers Yeovil Town. The Somerset club had defeated 2nd Division Bury and First Division Sunderland, with the 5th round taking them to Manchester. But they met their match with the Reds, losing 8-0 on February 12th 1949, in a game where Burke scored twice, Mitten once, and Rowley netted an amazing five goals.

In round six United defeated Hull 1-0, the semi-final against Wolves resulting in a 1-1 draw on March 26th. Unfortunately, in the replay at Goodison Park, United lost 1-0.

In August 1949, the Reds returned to Old Trafford after an absence of 8 years, during which time the débris of bomb damage had been cleared away and new buildings erected. The first home game on 24 August culminated in a 3-0 victory against Bolton, with Charlie Mitten scoring the first goal at Old Trafford in eight years.

The close of the 1949/50 season saw United finish fourth in Division One as fans pondered over what the next decade would hold for the club.

League Success –
Youth Policy Pays Off

United finished runners up in the 1950/1 League table, with this season seeing the signing of talented Johnny Berry for £25,000 from Birmingham City. The clever outside right caused problems for many defences during his 273 games with United, contributing 44 goals between 1951 and 1958. Sadly the injuries sustained at the Munich crash curtailed the career of a player who had won four England caps and three championship medals with the Reds.

The 1951/52 season is unforgettable for United fans. In the first two games on August 18th and August 22nd 1951, Rowley scored a hat trick in each! The initial confrontation with West Bromwich ended in a 3-3 draw, and the next game saw Middlesbrough defeated 4-2, United goals coming from Pearson and Rowley.

Of course, the climax of this season was United's Championship win for the first time in 40 years. The young side was determined to secure top place in Division One in spite of strenuous efforts by Arsenal who were battling to win the League and Cup double.

In the penultimate game of the season, the Reds defeated Chelsea 3-0. The last game was against Arsenal who had been United's main rivals for most of the season. The exciting last League match of 1951/2 took place on April 26th at Old Trafford with a crowd of over 53,000 willing their team to win. The result was a conclusive 6-1 victory for United, with goals by courtesy of Jack Rowley (3), Stan Pearson (2) and Roger Byrne. Those who attended this game can never forget the drama and terrific goals which reinforced United's place at the top of Division One, and reminded people of the team's fearsome attacking prowess.

The "Busby Babes"

The 1952/3 season finished with United placed eighth and City 20th in the First Division, and Matt Busby was clearly anxious to introduce younger players in his squad.

The team now offered an interesting blend of old and young, as typified by those who played in Round 5 of the FA Cup on February 14th 1953 – Wood, Aston, Byrne, Chilton, Carey, Cockburn, Berry, Lewis, Rowley, Pearson, Pegg. Some years earlier, in the 1948 FA Cup Final, when the Reds defeated Blackpool 4-2, Carey, Chilton, Rowley, Cochburn and Pearson were in the squad. In fact Johnny Carey had played in every position for United except outside left when he finally departed from the club in 1953.

In a friendly game against Kilmarnock, Matt Busby and Jimmy Murphy tried out a young team including David Pegg, Duncan Edwards, Eddie Colman and Wilf McGuiness.

The 3-0 victory convinced everyone that Busby's scheme had paid off and United won the FA Youth Cup Final each year between 1953 and 1957. Of course maestro Tommy Taylor arrived in 1952/3 following a payment of £29,999 to Barnsley, the talented player scoring 7 goals in his first 11 games. This fee was agreed in order to prevent his being tagged "A £30,000 player"! Local lad Dennis Viollet signed on in 1953 at the age of 16, staying with Old Trafford until he moved to Stoke in 1962.

With an average age of 22, the United squad who won the League title was one of the youngest sides to achieve this honour. The First Divison League positions between 1952 and 1957 underline the success of Busby's youth policy:

FIRST DIVISION RESULTS 1951 – 52

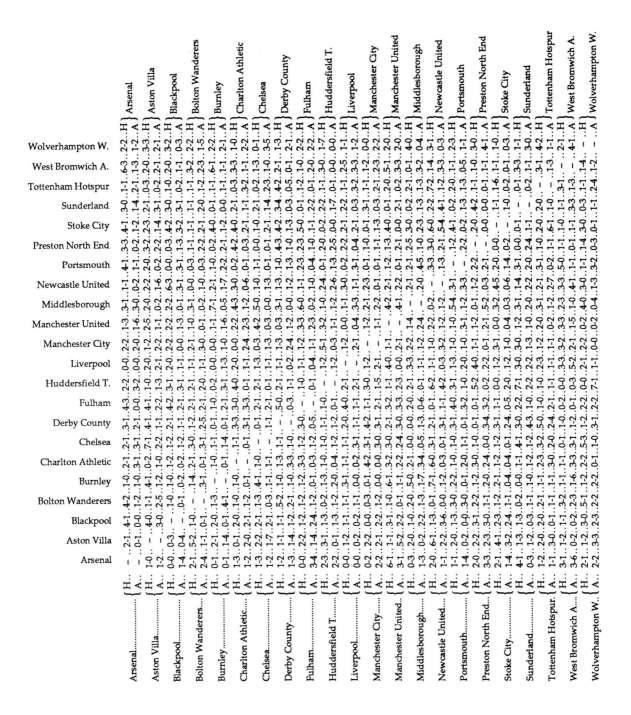

Drama from a game on 23rd December 1950 as
United tackle Bolton Wanderers, the latter winning
3–2. The Manchester club's goals were supplied
by Aston and Pearson.

FIRST DIVISION FINAL POSITIONS 1951-52

	P.	Home					Away					Pts.
		W.	D.	L.	F.	A.	W.	D.	L.	F.	A.	
Manchester United...	42	15	3	3	55	21	8	8	5	40	31	57
Tottenham Hotspur..	42	16	1	4	45	20	6	8	7	31	31	53
Arsenal........................	42	13	7	1	54	30	8	4	9	26	31	53
Portsmouth...............	42	13	3	5	42	25	7	5	9	26	33	48
Bolton Wanderers.....	42	11	7	3	35	26	8	3	10	30	35	48
Aston Villa.................	42	13	3	5	49	28	6	6	9	30	42	47
Preston North End....	42	10	5	6	39	22	7	7	7	35	32	46
Newcastle United......	42	12	4	5	62	28	6	5	10	36	45	45
Blackpool..................	42	12	5	4	40	27	6	4	11	24	37	45
Charlton Athletic.......	42	12	5	4	41	24	5	5	11	27	39	44
Liverpool..................	42	6	11	4	31	25	6	8	7	26	36	43
Sunderland...............	42	8	6	7	41	28	7	6	8	29	33	42
West Bromich A........	42	8	9	4	38	29	6	4	11	36	48	41
Burnley......................	42	9	6	6	32	19	6	4	11	24	44	40
Manchester City........	42	7	5	9	29	28	6	8	7	29	33	39
Wolverhampton W...	42	8	6	7	40	33	4	8	9	33	40	38
Derby County...........	42	10	4	7	43	37	5	3	13	20	43	37
Middlesborough.......	42	12	4	5	37	25	3	2	16	27	63	36
Chelsea......................	42	10	3	8	31	29	4	5	12	21	43	36
Stoke City.................	42	8	6	7	34	32	4	1	16	15	56	31
Huddersfield Town..	42	9	3	9	32	35	1	5	15	17	47	28
Fulham......................	42	5	7	9	38	31	3	4	14	20	46	27

ANALYSIS OF MANCHESTER UNITED'S LEAGUE MATCHES, 1951-52

Played 42...........	Won	23	(15 at home; 8 away)
	Drew	11	(3 at home; 8 away)
	Lost	8	(3 at home; 5 away)

Goals for......................... 95 (55 at home; 40 away)
Goals against................. 52 (21 at home; 31 away)
Points .... 57 out of a possible 84

AT HOME

1 match won   1-0 ⎫
2 matches won   2-1 ⎬ 5 by 1 goal
2 matches won   3-2 ⎭

2 matches won   2-0 ⎫
1 match won   3-1 ⎬ 4 by 2 goals
1 match won   4-2 ⎭

1 match won   3-0

5 matches won by more than 3 goals

3 matches drawn 1-1

1 match lost   0-1 ⎫
1 match lost   1-2 ⎬ 2 by 1 goal
1 match lost   1-3 ⎭

AWAY

3 matches won   2-1   (3 by 1 goal)

2 matches won   2-0 ⎫
1 match won   3-1 ⎬ 2 by 2 goals

1 match won   3-0 ⎫
1 match won   4-1 ⎬ 3 by 3 goals
1 match won   5-2 ⎭

2 matches drawn   0-0
1 match drawn   1-1
3 matches drawn   2-2
2 matches drawn   3-3

2 matches lost   0-1 ⎫
1 match lost   2-3 ⎬ 3 by 1 goal
1 match lost   0-2 ⎫
1 match lost   2-4 ⎬ 2 by 2 goals

YEAR	POSITION/TEAM
1952/3	1st Arsenal
	8th Manchester United
1953/4	1st Wolves
	4th Manchester United
1954/5	1st Chelsea
	5th Manchester United
1955/6	1st Manchester United
1956/7	1st Manchester United

United were clearly a force to be reckoned with, reaching an unassailable position at the top of the table in two consecutive seasons.

In 1955/6 the Reds were unbeaten at home and displayed an 11 point advantage over runners-up, Blackpool. A score of 60 points from 42 First Division matches had been equalled on several occasions, but the 11 point margin had only twice been reached.

In the mid 1950s, Manchester United proved themselves to be one of the finest teams of the decade, playing with ability and determination. To cite just one instance of the club's success at this period of time, they became League champions in 1956 for the fourth time in their history, and the second time since the War. Naturally, the supporters flocked to see their team, as shown by the attendance at an important League game against Blackpool in April 1956. The Old Trafford gates were closed 30 minutes before the kick off, as a new post war record crowd of 62,277 waited for the Red's 2-1 win.

The year is 1955 as Old Trafford crowds witness this Moir shot, which followed a back header by the celebrated Nat Lofthouse. Playing on January 22nd, Bolton held the Manchester club to a 1–1 draw, with the Reds having their goal supplied by Taylor.

FIRST DIVISION RESULTS 1955 – 56

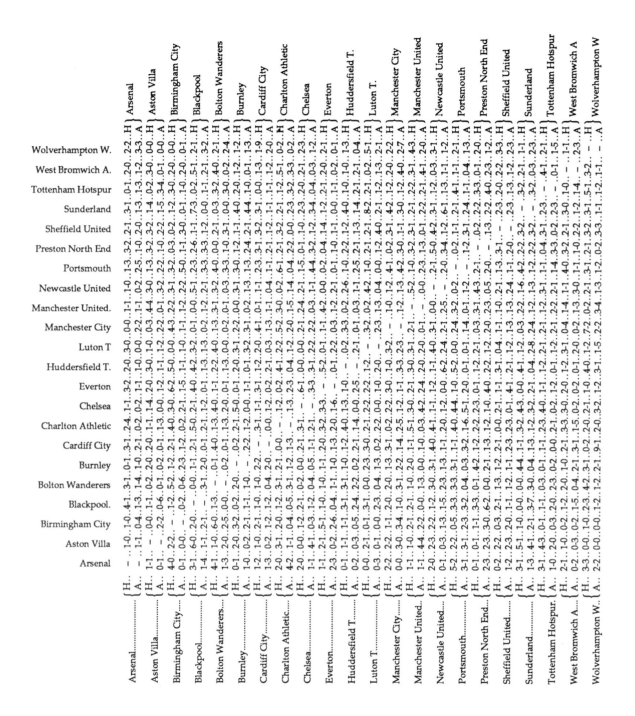

FIRST DIVISION FINAL POSITIONS 1956-57

	P.	Home					Away					Total		
		W.	D.	L.	F.	A.	W.	D.	L.	F.	A.	F.	A.	Pts.
Manchester United...	42	14	4	3	55	25	14	4	3	48	29	103	54	64
Tottenham Hotspur..	42	15	4	2	70	24	7	8	6	34	32	104	56	56
Preston North End....	42	15	4	2	50	19	8	6	7	34	37	84	56	56
Blackpool..................	42	14	3	4	55	26	8	6	7	38	39	93	65	53
Arsenal.....................	42	12	5	4	45	21	9	3	9	40	48	85	69	50
Wolverhampton W...	42	17	2	2	70	29	3	6	12	24	41	94	70	48
Burnley.....................	42	14	5	2	41	21	4	5	12	15	29	56	50	46
Leeds United............	42	10	8	3	42	18	5	6	10	30	45	72	63	44
Bolton Wanderers.....	42	13	6	2	42	23	3	6	12	23	42	65	65	44
Aston Villa................	42	10	8	3	45	25	4	7	10	20	30	65	55	43
West Bromich A........	42	8	8	5	31	25	6	6	9	28	36	59	61	42
Birmingham City.......	42	12	5	4	52	25	3	4	14	17	44	69	69	*39
Chelsea.....................	42	7	8	6	43	36	6	5	10	30	37	73	73	*39
Sheffield Wednesday	42	14	3	4	55	29	2	3	16	27	59	82	88	38
Everton.....................	42	10	5	6	34	28	4	5	12	27	51	61	79	38
Luton Town...............	42	10	4	7	32	26	4	5	12	26	50	58	76	37
Newcastle United......	42	10	5	6	43	31	4	3	14	24	56	67	87	36
Manchester City........	42	10	2	9	48	42	3	7	11	30	46	78	88	35
Portsmouth...............	42	8	6	7	37	35	2	7	12	25	57	62	92	33
Sunderland................	42	9	5	7	40	30	3	3	15	27	58	67	88	32
Cardiff City...............	42	7	6	8	35	34	3	3	15	18	54	53	88	29
Charlton Athletic.......	42	7	3	11	31	44	2	1	18	31	76	62	120	22

* Equal

ANALYSIS OF MANCHESTER UNITED'S LEAGUE MATCHES, 1955-56

Played 42............ Won 25 (18 at home; 7 away)

Drew 10 (3 at home; 7 away)

Lost 7 (0 at home; 7 away)

Goals for......................... 83 (51 at home; 32 away)

Goals against................. 51 (20 at home; 31 away)

Points .... 60 out of a possible 84

AT HOME

3 matches won 1-0 ⎫

5 matches won 2-1 ⎬ 10 by 1 goal

1 match won 3-2 ⎪

1 match won 4-3 ⎭

1 match won 2-0 ⎫ 4 by 2 goals

3 matches won 3-1 ⎭

2 matches won 3-0 ⎫ 3 by 3 goals

1 match won 5-2 ⎭

1 match won 5-1 1 by 4 goals

2 matches drawn 1-1

1 match drawn 2-2

No matches lost

AWAY

1 match won 1-0 ⎫ 2 by 1 goal

1 match won 2-1 ⎭

3 matches won 2-0 ⎫ 4 by 2 goals

1 match won 4-2 ⎭

1 match won 4-1 1 by 3 goals

3 matches drawn 0-0

1 match drawn 1-1

2 matches drawn 2-2

1 matches drawn 4-4

2 matches lost 0-1 ⎫ 3 by 1 goal

1 match lost 2-3 ⎭

2 matches lost 1-3 ⎫ 3 by 2 goals

1 match lost 2-4 ⎭

1 match lost 0-3 1 by 3 goals

Attendance at home matches: 818,498 = Average : 38,976

Attraction at away matches: 688,139 = Average : 32,768

Attendance at home Cup-ties: None at home

Best home gate: 62,277 *v.* Blackpool

FIRST DIVISION RESULTS 1956 – 57

		Arsenal	Aston Villa	Birmingham City	Blackpool.	Bolton Wanderers	Burnley	Cardiff City	Charlton Athletic	Chelsea	Everton	Leeds United	Luton T	Manchester City	Manchester United.	Newcastle United	Portsmouth	Preston North End	Sheffield Wednesday	Sunderland	Tottenham Hotspur	West Bromwich A.	Wolverhampton W.		
Arsenal	H	–	2-1	4-0	1-1	3-0	2-0	0-0	3-1	2-0	2-0	1-0	1-3	7-3	1-2	0-1	1-1	1-2	6-3	1-1	3-1	4-1	0-0	H	Arsenal
	A	–	0-0	2-4	4-2	1-2	1-3	3-2	3-1	1-1	0-4	3-3	2-1	3-2	2-6	1-3	3-2	0-3	4-2	0-1	3-1	2-0	2-5	A	
Aston Villa	H	0-0	–	3-1	3-2	0-0	1-0	4-1	3-1	1-1	5-1	1-1	1-3	2-2	1-3	3-1	2-2	2-0	5-0	2-2	2-4	0-0	4-0	H	Aston Villa
	A	1-2	–	2-1	0-0	0-0	1-2	0-1	2-0	1-1	4-0	0-1	0-0	1-1	1-1	2-1	1-5	3-3	1-2	0-1	0-3	0-2	0-3	A	
Birmingham City	H	4-2	1-2	–	2-2	0-0	2-0	2-1	4-2	0-1	1-3	6-2	3-0	3-3	3-1	6-1	3-1	3-0	4-0	1-2	0-0	2-0	2-2	H	Birmingham City
	A	0-4	1-3	–	1-3	1-3	0-2	2-1	0-1	0-1	0-2	1-1	0-0	1-3	2-2	2-3	4-3	0-1	0-3	1-0	1-5	0-0	0-3	A	
Blackpool	H	2-4	0-0	3-1	–	4-2	1-0	3-1	3-2	1-0	5-2	1-1	4-0	4-1	2-2	2-3	5-0	4-0	3-1	1-2	4-1	0-1	3-2	H	Blackpool
	A	1-1	2-3	2-2	–	1-4	2-2	4-3	4-0	2-2	3-2	0-5	2-0	3-0	2-0	1-2	0-0	0-0	2-1	2-5	1-2	3-1	1-4	A	
Bolton Wanderers	H	2-1	0-0	3-1	4-1	–	3-0	2-0	2-0	2-2	1-1	5-3	2-2	1-0	2-0	3-1	1-0	2-3	3-2	2-1	1-0	1-1	0-3	H	Bolton Wanderers
	A	0-3	0-0	0-0	2-4	–	0-1	0-2	1-2	2-2	2-2	2-3	0-1	3-1	2-0	0-4	1-0	2-2	2-1	0-3	0-4	2-3	2-3	A	
Burnley	H	3-1	2-1	2-0	2-2	1-0	–	6-2	2-1	2-0	2-1	0-0	1-1	0-3	1-3	3-2	1-0	2-2	4-1	2-0	1-0	1-0	3-0	H	Burnley
	A	0-2	0-1	0-2	0-1	0-3	–	3-3	2-1	0-2	0-1	1-1	2-0	1-0	0-2	1-1	0-1	0-1	0-0	1-2	0-2	2-2	2-1	A	
Cardiff City	H	2-3	1-0	1-2	3-4	2-0	3-3	–	2-3	1-1	1-0	4-1	0-0	1-1	2-3	5-2	0-2	2-3	2-1	1-0	0-3	0-0	2-2	H	Cardiff City
	A	0-0	1-4	1-2	1-3	0-2	2-6	–	2-0	2-1	0-0	0-3	0-3	1-4	1-3	0-1	0-1	0-6	3-5	1-1	0-5	2-1	1-3	A	
Charlton Athletic	H	1-3	0-2	1-0	0-4	2-1	1-2	0-2	–	3-1	1-2	1-2	1-2	1-0	1-5	1-1	1-3	3-4	4-4	3-2	1-1	3-2	2-1	H	Charlton Athletic
	A	1-3	1-3	2-4	2-3	0-2	1-2	3-2	–	3-1	0-5	0-4	2-4	1-5	2-4	1-3	0-1	3-4	1-3	1-8	2-6	2-2	3-7	A	
Chelsea	H	1-1	1-1	1-0	2-2	2-2	2-0	1-2	1-3	–	5-1	1-1	4-1	4-2	1-2	6-2	3-3	1-0	0-0	0-2	2-4	2-4	3-3	H	Chelsea
	A	0-2	1-1	1-0	0-1	2-2	0-2	1-1	1-3	–	3-0	0-0	4-0	4-5	0-3	2-1	2-2	0-1	0-4	3-1	4-3	1-2	1-3	A	
Everton	H	4-0	0-4	2-0	2-3	2-2	1-0	0-0	5-0	0-3	–	2-1	2-1	1-1	1-2	2-1	2-2	1-4	1-0	2-1	1-1	0-1	3-1	H	Everton
	A	0-2	1-5	3-1	2-5	1-1	1-2	0-1	2-1	1-5	–	1-5	0-2	4-2	5-2	0-0	2-3	0-0	2-2	1-1	0-6	0-3	1-2	A	
Leeds United	H	3-3	1-0	1-1	5-0	3-2	1-1	3-0	4-0	0-0	5-1	–	1-2	2-0	1-2	0-0	4-1	1-2	3-1	3-1	1-1	0-0	0-0	H	Leeds United
	A	0-1	1-1	2-6	1-1	3-5	0-0	1-4	2-1	1-1	1-2	–	2-2	0-1	2-3	3-2	5-2	0-3	3-2	0-2	1-5	0-0	2-1	A	
Luton T.	H	1-2	0-0	0-0	0-2	1-0	0-2	3-0	4-2	0-4	2-0	2-2	–	3-2	0-2	4-1	1-0	1-1	2-0	6-2	1-3	0-1	1-0	H	Luton T.
	A	3-1	3-1	0-3	0-4	2-2	1-1	0-0	2-1	1-4	1-2	2-1	–	2-3	1-3	2-2	2-2	0-2	0-3	0-1	0-5	0-4	4-5	A	
Manchester City	H	2-3	1-1	3-1	0-3	1-3	0-1	4-1	5-1	5-4	2-4	1-0	3-2	–	2-4	1-2	5-1	0-2	4-2	3-1	2-2	2-1	2-3	H	Manchester City
	A	3-7	2-2	3-3	1-4	0-1	3-0	1-1	0-1	2-4	1-1	0-2	2-3	–	0-2	3-0	1-0	1-3	2-2	1-1	2-3	1-1	1-5	A	
Manchester United.	H	6-2	1-1	2-2	0-2	0-2	2-0	3-1	4-2	3-0	2-5	3-2	3-1	2-0	–	6-1	3-0	3-2	4-1	4-0	0-0	1-1	3-0	H	Manchester United
	A	2-1	3-1	1-3	2-2	0-2	3-1	3-2	5-1	2-1	2-1	2-1	2-0	4-2	–	1-1	3-1	3-1	1-2	3-1	2-2	3-2	1-1	A	
Newcastle United	H	3-1	1-2	3-2	2-1	4-0	1-1	1-0	3-1	1-2	0-0	2-3	2-2	0-3	1-1	–	2-1	1-2	1-2	6-2	2-2	5-2	2-1	H	Newcastle United
	A	1-0	1-3	1-6	3-2	1-3	2-3	2-5	1-1	2-6	1-2	0-0	1-4	2-1	1-6	–	2-2	0-1	0-4	2-1	1-3	0-1	0-2	A	
Portsmouth	H	2-3	5-1	3-4	0-0	1-1	1-0	1-0	1-0	2-2	3-2	2-5	2-2	0-1	1-3	2-2	–	2-2	3-1	3-2	2-3	0-1	1-0	H	Portsmouth
	A	1-1	2-2	1-3	0-5	1-1	1-1	2-0	3-1	3-3	2-2	1-4	0-1	1-5	0-3	1-2	–	1-7	1-3	3-3	0-2	1-2	0-6	A	
Preston North End	H	3-0	3-3	1-0	0-0	2-2	1-0	6-0	4-3	1-0	0-0	3-0	2-0	3-1	1-3	1-0	7-1	–	1-0	6-0	1-4	3-2	1-0	H	Preston North End
	A	2-1	0-2	0-3	0-4	3-2	2-2	3-2	4-3	0-1	4-1	2-1	1-1	2-0	2-3	2-1	2-2	–	1-3	0-0	1-1	0-0	3-4	A	
Sheffield Wednesday	H	2-4	2-1	3-0	1-2	1-2	0-0	5-3	3-1	4-0	2-2	2-3	3-0	2-2	2-1	4-0	3-1	3-1	–	3-2	4-1	4-2	2-1	H	Sheffield Wednesday
	A	3-6	0-5	0-4	1-3	2-3	1-4	1-2	4-4	0-0	0-1	1-3	0-2	2-4	1-4	2-1	1-3	0-1	–	2-5	1-1	4-1	1-2	A	
Sunderland	H	1-0	1-0	0-1	5-2	3-0	2-1	1-1	8-1	1-3	1-1	2-0	1-0	1-1	1-3	1-2	3-3	0-0	5-2	–	0-2	1-4	2-3	H	Sunderland
	A	1-1	2-2	2-1	2-1	1-2	0-2	0-1	2-3	2-0	1-2	1-3	2-6	1-3	0-4	2-6	2-3	0-6	2-3	–	2-5	0-2	2-2	A	
Tottenham Hotspur.	H	1-3	3-0	5-1	2-1	4-0	2-0	5-0	6-2	3-4	6-0	5-1	5-0	3-2	2-2	3-1	2-0	1-1	1-1	5-2	–	2-2	4-1	H	Tottenham Hotspur
	A	1-3	4-2	0-0	1-4	0-1	0-1	3-0	1-1	4-2	1-1	1-1	3-1	2-2	0-0	2-2	3-2	4-1	1-4	2-0	–	1-1	0-3	A	
West Bromwich A	H	0-2	2-0	0-0	1-3	3-2	2-2	1-2	2-2	2-1	3-0	0-0	4-0	1-1	2-3	1-0	2-1	0-0	1-4	2-0	1-1	–	1-1	H	West Bromwich A
	A	1-4	0-0	0-2	1-0	1-1	0-1	0-0	2-3	4-2	1-0	0-0	1-0	1-2	1-1	2-5	1-0	2-3	2-4	4-1	2-2	–	2-5	A	
Wolverhampton W.	H	5-2	3-0	3-0	4-1	3-2	1-2	3-1	7-3	3-1	2-1	1-2	5-4	5-1	1-1	2-0	6-0	4-3	2-1	2-2	3-0	5-2	–	H	Wolverhampton W
	A	0-0	0-4	2-2	2-3	3-0	0-3	2-2	1-2	3-3	1-3	0-0	0-1	3-2	0-3	1-2	0-1	0-1	1-2	3-2	1-4	1-1	–	A	

Bobby Charlton and the elusive Triple

The 1956/7 season will always be considered a great period in the club's history, with the Reds reaching the Final of the FA Cup, becoming leaders of Division One and taking part in the European Cup. Evening matches would now be enjoyed by courtesy of new floodlighting, details of which were announced in August 1956. United were to spend over £40,000 on installing four 160 feet steel towers each containing 54 floodlights.

Bobby Charlton

One man who was to figure prominently in the crucial games of this season was Bobby Charlton, whose initial first team appearance for the Reds took place on October 6th 1956. Playing with the club for 17 seasons, this gentleman of soccer took part in over 600 League games, 79 FA Cup Matches, 24 Football League Cup games, and 45 European Cup matches.

This superlative player was a tremendous performer in his own right, displaying natural stamina and flawless moves as he threatened opposing defences in England and overseas when he represented his country.

We all know that on trips abroad, any reference to "Manchester" frequently evokes the rejoinder, "Manchester United, Bobby Charlton". This ambassador of the game never lost his temper on the pitch, and his skill and shooting powers will long remain in our minds. Those of us fortunate enough to see Bobby play will surely remember his humility, sincerity, dignity and unsurpassed skill.

This natural player scored 247 goals for the club and was the recipient of 106 England caps.

And so back to the 1956/7 season when United's trophies included the FA Youth Cup and the FA Charity Shield.

The Triple

1. The League

The Reds won the First Division for the second year in succession:

	P	W	D	L	F	A	Pts
1955/56							
1st Manchester United	42	25	10	7	83	51	60
2nd Blackpool	42	20	9	13	86	62	49
1956/57							
1st Manchester United	42	28	8	6	103	54	64
2nd Tottenham	42	22	12	8	104	56	56

Not surprisingly, Bobby Charlton made an impact on these results, scoring twice in his début first team match at Old Trafford on October 6th 1956. The 4-2 win over (interestingly) Charlton Athletic came about from two goals by Bobby and a goal each from Whelan and Berry. United by now had emerged as the most effective side since the War, with outside forwards Pegg and Berry delivering lightning strikes on unsuspecting defences. The usual team-mates on the forward line at this period were Whelan, Viollet, Charlton and Taylor, while Colman and Edwards at wing half sent many useful balls to the forward line.

2. The 1957 FA Cup

United reached Wembley in this memorable season by tackling a variety of teams from a number of divisions:

DATE	OPPONENTS	SCORE
January 5th	Hartlepool United	4-3
January 26th	Wrexham	5-0
February 16th	Everton	1-0
March 2nd	Bournemouth & Boscombe A.	2-1
March 23rd (Semi-Final)	Birmingham	2-0

These were not straight-forward games and posed several anxious moments for United fans. For example in the game of January 5th, the Reds were ahead at one stage by three goals to nil, while the Everton match saw some strong resistance from the Merseysiders until Edwards' goal put United into the next round.

The quarter final against Bournemouth, certainly took supporters by surprise with United trailing 1-0 at half time. They were eventually saved by Johnny Berry's two goals. In the semi-final, it was Berry again plus Bobby Charlton who provided the winners.

In April 1957 there was guarded optimism in the United camp. That month would bring the European Cup semi-final, followed by the FA Cup Final in May.

On the 4th May 1957, United and Aston Villa took to the Wembley arena, where Jackie Blanchflower and Bobby Charlton replaced the injured Jones and Viollet. Football aficionados on the terraces reminded friends that Aston Villa was the last team to achieve a double in 1897, and so the scene was set for the Final. The match opened with promise, each team providing cautious initial attacks.

One of the most unforgettable moments of the game was the awful collision between goalkeeper Ray Wood and Villa winger Peter McParland in the sixth minute. The United player was stretchered off with a fractured cheekbone as Blanchflower took over in the nets. The subsequent reshuffle meant that Duncan Edwards assumed the rôle of centre half as the ten men valiantly prevented Villa from scoring in the first three quarters of an hour.

Eventually the Midlands team produced two goals, both by McParland, United responding with a Tommy Taylor consolation goal seven minutes before the final whistle. Ray Wood came on in the closing minutes but, sadly, United's dream of the double finished as the 90 minute score line read: Aston Villa 2, Manchester United 1. The 100,000 crowd enjoyed a thrilling game, but one wonders what would have happened if a substitute 'keeper had been allowed to come on in 1957? Full credit to the team of Wood, Foulkes, Byrne, Colman, Blanchflower, Berry, Edwards, Whelan, Taylor, Charlton, and Pegg, who displayed matchless energy and determination.

The lithe and agile Bill Foulkes heads clear as Lofthouse surges towards the United goal in the 1958 FA Cup final at Wembley.

3. The European Cup

Talk to any United supporter of the late 1950s and he will quote the run up to the European Cup. In September 1956, the Preliminary Rounds witnessed the Reds emerge as victors with an unbelievable win of 12-0 on aggregate over two legs!

First Leg – September 12th 1956
R.S.C. Anderlecht 0 – Manchester United 2

What a great event for team and supporters alike as the club's first competitive game in Europe took place in Brussels. Dennis Viollet and Tommy Taylor outwitted the Anderlecht keeper and everyone looked forward to the next encounter.

Second Leg – September 26th 1956
R.S.C. Anderlecht 0 – Manchester United 10
(Aggregate 12-0)

Who in Manchester, or even Europe, can ever forget this return tie against Anderlecht, played at Maine Road? (Old Trafford's floodlights were not yet in use). A wild crowd of 40,000 ignored the murky weather as 10 goals were hammered into the Belgian net. In the first half alone Tommy Taylor put 2 goals away, while Dennis Viollet scored a hat trick!

After the interval, Taylor completed his own hat trick, followed by a goal from Whelan, while another from Viollet made it 8-0. A Berry goal, plus a second from Whelan completed the rout of Anderlecht. If one were to single out a "Man of the Match", it would have to be David Pegg, who engineered most of the goals, reminding everyone that his reading of the game was legendary.

Now agog with excitement, the Manchester fans eagerly awaited subsequent games in the European Cup.

Sadly, United lost the tie with Real Madrid, 5-3 on

Date	Opponents	Game	Score
Oct 17th	Borussia Dortmund	Round 1 First Leg	W. 3-2
Nov 21st	Borussia Dortmund	Round 2 Second Leg	D. 0-0
Jan 16th	Atletico Bilbao	Quarter Final 1st Leg	L. 3-5
Feb 6th	Atletico Bilbao (Agg.6-5)	Quarter Final. 2nd Leg	W. 3-0
Apr 11th	Real Madrid	Semi-final 1st Leg	L. 1-3
Apr 25th	Real Madrid (Agg.3-5)	Semi-final. 2nd Leg	D. 2-2

aggregate, but this was nothing of which the Reds should have been ashamed. Real Madrid boasted such distinguished stars as di Stefano, Riall, Puskas and Kopa. The pressures on Matt Busby and the team were tremendous in Spring 1957, but the club and players fully enjoyed what was their finest hour of the 1950s.

In 1956/7, United were way ahead of all their rivals. Not only were they close to picking up the League and Cup "Double", but also performing so admirably in the European Cup. Right from the outset, they quickly demonstrated they had the ability to repeat the previous season's victory. Apart from a short spell when Spurs showed their skills, United stayed at the top of Division One for almost all season, thanks to their tough and consistent approach to the game.

Look at what supporters had to pay at Old Trafford in 1959. Entrance to the Paddock and Terrace was three shillings and sixpence, when a shilling was equivalent to today's 5p.

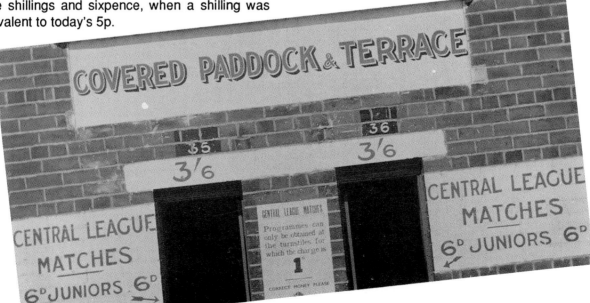

What a near miss in the 1958 FA Cup Final! The ball skims past the post with Bolton's 'keeper, Hopkinson, looking on, while United's Dennis Viollet is ready to pounce

Brian Edwards blocks a shot by Viollet and the ball
goes over the line for a corner in the 1958 FA Cup
Final

Full back Tony Dunne, (wearing a number two shirt), was a tireless defender who played over 500 games for the Reds between 1960 and 1973.

Munich

As League champions of 1956/7, United were entitled to a second crack at the European Cup, so, following an aggregate victory of 9-2 over Shamrock Rovers, the Reds took on Dukla Prague, resulting in an overall win of 3-1 for the English club.

The European Cup Quarter Finals featured Yugoslavian champions Red Star Belgrade, the First Leg taking place on January 14th 1958 at Old Trafford. The home team won 2-1 thanks to goals by Colman and Charlton. Ardent United fans will recall the nine goals scored in the 5-4 "Busby Babes" victory over Arsenal on February 1st, and this whetted the appetite for February 5th when the quarter final (2nd Leg) of the European Cup would take place against Red Star Belgrade.

The team comprised: Gregg, Byrne, Foulkes, Colman, Edwards, Jones, Morgans, Charlton, Taylor, Viollet, Scanlon.

Failed take-off

Following a 5-4 aggregate victory, the team headed for home. The United party, together with other passengers who included 11 British journalists, boarded an aircraft on 6th February 1958. The plane landed at Munich to refuel and following two attempts to take off, a third try was made at 3.03 pm on that sad February day. The rest is history. The aircraft veered off the runway amid slush and snow and then hit a house.

Players who perished immediately were David Pegg, Tommy Taylor, Roger Byrne, Geoff Bent, Eddie Colman, Liam Whelan and Mark Jones. The same fate came to secretary Walter Crickmer, coach Herbert Whalley and trainer Tom Curry. Eight journalists and three other passengers also lost their lives in the incident. Duncan Edwards died two weeks later.

Those sustaining injuries included Matt Busby, Johnny Berry, Jackie Blanchflower, Bobby Charlton and Dennis Viollet.

The depressing events stunned the soccer world. Everyone wondered if United would ever be the same again, as Jimmy Murphy faced a huge task of reconstructing the side.

He had been on Welsh management duties in Cardiff on that fateful day. Of the survivors, only Harry Gregg and Bill Foulkes could immediately take up first team duties.

Post-Munich

The scheduled League game against Wolves was postponed while Jimmy Murphy acted shrewdly and smartly, signing the impressive Ernie Taylor and Stan Crowther. Jimmy was now relying on his talented young stars who included Alex Dawson, Mark Peason, Shay Brennan, Ronnie Cope, Ian Greaves and Colin Webster.

The world of soccer waited anxiously for United's first game. How would the new side perform? February 19th was the date. The occasion – fifth round of the FA Cup against Sheffield Wednesday. A crowd of 59,000 witnessed a 3-0 victory for the Reds, while the next League game at home took place on 22nd February. The score was a 1-1 draw with Nottingham Forest.

In the European Cup, the Reds were defeated by AC Milàn 5-2 on aggregate, although the Old Trafford game had produced a 2-1 victory for United. The FA Cup Final brought a 2-0 defeat by Bolton, where Nat Lofthouse scored both goals. The close of the 1957/8 season saw the Reds placed ninth in Division One.

Always on hand to fend off the opposition, Nobby Stiles, (extreme right), looks on as a Norwich City attack is about to commence. This piece of action comes from Round Four of the F.A. Cup on February 18th, 1967 when United lost 1–2, their only goal coming from Denis Law.

New Signings – famous names

It was impossible to forget the tragedy which befell the Manchester club in 1958, but life had to go on at Old Trafford. The next season saw Matt Busby resume his duties as manager, now recovered from his Munich injuries. He introduced Warren Bradley and Albert Quixall to the squad, the former a teacher and international amateur player who was signed from Bishop Auckland. Quixall moved from Sheffield Wednesday for a £45,000 fee, remaining at Old Trafford until 1964, while Bradley left two years earlier. Tony Dunne made his début in 1960, giving unstinting service until his move to Bolton Wanderers in 1973.

Nobby Stiles

Hailing from Manchester's Collyhurst district, Nobby played his first League game for United in October 1960, when he was 18 years of age. The fiery youngster had joined the club as a schoolboy three years earlier and he turned out to be a hard, resilient player, teaming up with Bill Foulkes to form a strong defence.

Nobby made 392 appearances for the Reds and he gained 28 England caps before suffering cartilage problems in his late twenties. Moving to Middlesbrough in 1971, he then took up a number of posts before coming back to United in 1989 as Youth Team coach.

Denis Law

Denis signed for United from the Italian club Torino in 1962 for a then record fee of £115,000. This former Huddersfield Town and Manchester City star was to have a significant effect on United.

Denis Law, (right), in a typical position close to the opposition's goalmouth. He scored almost 240 goals for United between 1962 and 1973, and he was the recipient of several medals, being nominated European Player of the Year in 1964.

Law played in the Reds' FA Cup winning squad of 1963, and he received the European Player of the Year award 12 months later. The Scottish international was christened 'The King' by Old Trafford fans – not surprising as he scored 23 League goals in his first season with United, while 30 League games in 1963/4 produced an amazing 30 goals for him!

It was a thrilling spectacle to see him thundering down the pitch, running rings round perplexed defenders, while his rapport with fellow forward David Herd was to be the downfall of so many opposing teams.

To cite a couple instances of Denis' skills, how about his hat trick against Huddersfield in 1963 when the 5-0 victory set United on the Wembley trail. Again, the actual Final against Leicester City witnessed a superb Law goal in the 29th minute, the other two coming from David Herd.

One goal which United fans might prefer to forget occurred in 1974 after Law had joined Manchester City. Eight minutes from the end of a crucial game against United, Denis backheeled the ball past Alex Stepney to make the score 1-0 for City, thus forcing relegation on Law's old club.

Denis demonstrated unqualified dribbling skills and brilliant ball control, coupled with an intense love of the game. Today he is a respected sports commentator who is often seen and heard on television and radio.

George Best

Another great player who arrived at Old Trafford in the early 1960s, George Best played his first game for the Reds when he was $17^1/_2$ in September 1963. George quickly became the soccer hero of many fans.

Superlatives can only be used to describe a player whose hint of genius contributed so much to the United story. The complete footballer with a unique touch, George Best was both an innovator and thinker who departed from Old Trafford in 1974 after 466 games in League, FA Cup, Football League Cup and European competitions. The Northern Ireland international was a recipient of Footballer of the Year award in 1968, and was also given the European Player of the Year Trophy. He received Championship medals in 1965 and 1967.

His skill, daring and courage were second to none, paying dividends when it came to finding the back of the net. In the 1967/68 season,

George's name appeared on the score sheet 32 times with 28 goals coming in League games, one in the FA Cup, and three in European matches.

Today, George has established himself as an author and media personality with a wealth of soccer knowledge.

1963 FA Cup Final

Although United were 19th in Division One at the close of the 1962/3 season they took the FA Cup back to Old Trafford after defeating Leicester City 3-1. The score indicated how the League position is a notoriously poor guide when it comes to the FA Cup. Needless to say, Denis Law made valuable contributions, scoring five goals in the qualifying rounds and in the Final.

During the first 15 minutes we witnessed a confident Leicester, but then the Manchester club assumed control, with the first goal appearing on the hour, scored by Law who had received a square ball from Crerand.

Following the interval, Foulkes, Cantwell and Dunne quashed any challenges from the Leicester attack. Twelve minutes into the second half, Giles supplied Charlton with a long cross field pass, the second player volleying a shot at 'keeper Banks. It was too hard for him to hang on to and Herd pounced on the rebound, sending it into the net. Just five minutes from the end Herd also supplied the last goal of the match.

The 1964 Sunderland Saga

The Reds met Sunderland on three occasions during 1964 on the road to Wembley, with a draw on February 29th in Round Six necessitating a replay on March 4th. Even with extra time this resulted in 2 goals apiece. The FA Cup sixth round serial between United and Sunderland had its final instalment on March 9th. This second replay was held on Huddersfield Town's ground, Manchester winning 5-1 with all goals scored after half time.

The three meetings between the two sides were watched by an official aggregate of 165,379, with receipts totalling £30,598. Just for a change, ticket touts suffered badly before the last game with a 10 shilling (50p) ticket selling for as little as 5 shillings (25p).

George Best captured in a classic shooting position in the late 1960s. Three defenders look on helplessly as the football genius penetrates their ranks.

The Leeds Tussle

During the 1964/5 season, the talented trio of Best, Charlton and Law ravaged many opposing defences with audacious attacks. Fans of that period will remember a dynamic run of 15 League games without losing, as United marched on to secure the Division One title. Between 8th September and 28th November 1964, the Reds drew twice and won 13 consecutive games. Little wonder that crowds of 50,000 or 60,000 were commonplace.

What a season this turned out to be, as in Spring of 1965, United notched up seven wins in a row. Needless to say the club attained top position in Division One for the 1964/5 season, having lost only seven of the 42 games played!

This era will always stay in our minds as the one where Leeds and Manchester United were tough adversaries. Who can forget the closing days of the season with Leeds and United level on points with one game still in hand for the Reds. The Yorkshire club had finished their season with a draw against Birmingham, and although United lost their final game against Aston Villa, goal average decided the winner.

This is how the top of the 1964/5 Division One table looked:

	P.	W.	D.	L.	F.	A.	PTS.
1st Manchester United	42	26	9	7	89	39	61
2nd Leeds	42	26	9	7	83	52	61

United won by 0.686 of a goal!

The 1964/5 period heralded considerable success outside the League as United reached the semi-final of the Inter Cities Fairs' Cup and the semi-final of the FA Cup where once again Leeds were the opposition. The two clubs met on March 27th 1965 at Hillsborough, a 0-0 draw in the semi-final forcing another match at the City Ground, Nottingham, on March 31st. United lost 1-0 to Leeds and no doubt players of both teams were glad this season was over.

European Soccer Again

United were once more playing in the European Cup, and made it to the semi-finals of the FA Cup, finishing fourth in Division One at the close of the 1965/6 season.

Highlights in this period must include the European Cup. Preliminary rounds saw the Reds thrash Helsinki 9-2 and then defeat A.S.K. Vor-

wärts 5-1 on aggregate. The quarter finals will long be savoured by Mancunians who relive the opposition provided by the mighty Benfica. In the first meeting of these giants on February 2nd 1965, Herd, Law and Foulkes each scored a goal to put United 3-2 ahead. However, it was the second Leg of the quarter final which was such a terrific match, worthy of further description:

9th March 1966   Benfica 1 Manchester United 5

75,000 ebullient supporters gathered in Lisbon to witness what was to be an exhilarating contest, with the first 16 minutes bringing three goals! George Best headed in a free kick after six minutes, then he took on three defenders to secure a second goal in the 12th minute. Connelly found the back of the net as United's third goal crashed home.

Following an own goal by United, Crerand and Charlton provided goals 4 and 5, resulting in an impressive 90 minute score of 5-1.

Hectic Season

February and March 1966 were particularly busy times for United with League games and other important matches: Here are some extracts from the club's timetable:

DATE	OPPONENTS	COMPETITION	SCORE	ROUND/LEG
Feb 2nd	Benfica	European Cup	W 3-2	Quarter-final (1st leg)
Feb 12th	Rotherham Utd	FA Cup	D 0-0	Round 4
Feb 15th	Rotherham Utd.	FA Cup (replay)	W 1-0(AET)	Round 4
March 5th	Wolves	FA Cup	W 4-2	Round 5
March 9th	Benfica	European Cup	W 5-1	Quarter-final (2nd leg)
March 26th	Preston N.E	FA Cup	D 1-1	Round 6
March 30th	Preston N.E.	FA Cup (replay)	W 3-1	Round 6
(AET – After Extra Time)				

So what happened at the close of this hectic season? Surprisingly, the Reds were pushed out of the European Cup in the semi-final when they played FK Partizan Belgrade in April. Semi-final blues struck again when a 1-0 defeat by Everton in the FA Cup match meant the club did not reach Wembley.

F.A. CHALLENGE CUP WINNERS 1872 – 1963

1872 and 1874–92...	Kennington Oval	1895–1914..............	Crystal Palace
1873......................	Lillie Bridge	1915......................	Old Trafford, Manchester
1893......................	Fallowfield, Manchester	1920–1922..............	Stamford Bridge
1894......................	Everton	1923 to date............	Wembley

Year	Winners	Runners-Up	Score
1872....	Wanderers	Royal Engineers	1–0
1873....	Wanderers	Oxford University	2–0
1874....	Oxford University	Royal Engineers	2–0
1875....	Royal Engineers	Old Etonians	2–0 after 1-1 draw
1876....	Wanderers	Old Etonians	3–0 after 0-0 draw
1877....	Wanderers	Oxford University	2–0 during extra time
1878....	*Wanderers	Royal Engineers	3–1
1879....	Old Etonians	Clapham Rovers	1–0
1880....	Clapham Rovers	Oxford University	1–0
1881....	Old Carthusians	Old Etonians	3–0
1882....	Old Etonians	Blackburn Rovers	1–0
1883....	Blackburn Olympic	Old Etonians	2–1 during extra time
1884....	Blackburn Rovers	Queen's Park, Glasgow	2–1
1885....	Blackburn Rovers	Queen's Park, Glasgow	2–0
1886....	†Blackburn Rovers	West Bromwich Albion	2–0 after 0-0 draw
1887....	Aston Villa	West Bromwich Albion	2–0
1888....	West Bromwich Albion	Preston North End	2–1
1889....	Preston North End	Wolverhampton Wanderers	3–0
1890....	Blackburn Rovers	Sheffield Wednesday	6–1
1891....	Blackburn Rovers	Notts County	3–1
1892....	West Bromwich Albion	Aston Villa	3–0
1893....	Wolverhampton Wanderers	Everton	1–0
1894....	Notts County	Bolton Wanderers	4–1
1895....	Aston Villa	West Bromwich Albion	1–0
1896....	Sheffield Wednesday	Wolverhampton Wanderers	2–1
1897....	Aston Villa	Everton	3–2
1898....	Nottingham Forest	Derby County	3–1
1899....	Sheffield United	Derby County	4–1
1900....	Bury	Southampton	4–0
1901....	Tottenham Hotspur	Sheffield United	3–1 after 2-2 draw
1902....	Sheffield United	Southampton	2–1 after 1-1 draw
1903....	Bury	Derby County	6–0
1904....	Manchester City	Bolton Wanderers	1–0
1905....	Aston Villa	Newcastle United	2–0
1906....	Everton	Newcastle United	1–0
1907....	Sheffield Wednesday	Everton	2–1
1908....	Wolverhampton Wanderers	Newcastle United	3–1
1909....	Manchester United	Bristol City	1–0
1910....	Newcastle United	Barnsley	2–0 after 1-1 draw
1911....	Bradford City	Newcastle United	1–0 after 0-0 draw
1912....	Barnsley	West Bromwich Albion	1–0 after 0-0 draw
1913....	Aston Villa	Sunderland	1–0
1914....	Burnley	Liverpool	1–0
1915....	Sheffield United	Chelsea	3–0
1920....	Aston Villa	Huddersfield Town	1–0 during extra time
1921....	Tottenham Hotspur	Wolverhampton Wanderers	1–0
1922....	Huddersfield Town	Preston North End	1–0
1923....	Bolton Wanderers	West Ham United	2–0
1924....	Newcastle United	Aston Villa	2–0
1925....	Sheffield United	Cardiff City	1–0
1926....	Bolton Wanderers	Manchester City	1–0
1927....	Cardiff City	Arsenal	1–0
1928....	Blackburn Rovers	Huddersfield Town	3–1
1929....	Bolton Wanderers	Portsmouth	2–0
1930....	Arsenal	Huddersfield Town	2–0
1931....	West Bromwich Albion	Birmingham	2–1
1932....	Newcastle United	Arsenal	2–1
1933....	Everton	Manchester City	3–0
1934....	Manchester City	Portsmouth	2–1
1935....	Sheffield Wednesday	West Bromwich Albion	4–2
1936....	Arsenal	Sheffield United	1–0
1937....	Sunderland	Preston North End	3–1
1938....	Preston North End	Huddersfield Town	1–0 during extra time
1939....	Portsmouth	Wolverhampton Wanderers	4–1
1946....	Derby County	Charlton Athletic	4–1 during extra time
1947....	Charlton Athletic	Burnley	1–0 during extra time
1948....	Manchester United	Blackpool	4–2
1949....	Wolverhampton Wanderers	Leicester City	3–1
1950....	Arsenal	Liverpool	2–0
1951....	Newcastle United	Blackpool	2–0
1952....	Newcastle United	Arsenal	1–0
1953....	Blackpool	Bolton Wanderers	4–3
1954....	West Bromwich Albion	Preston North End	3–2
1955....	Newcastle United	Manchester City	3–1
1956....	Manchester City	Birmingham City	3–1
1957....	Aston Villa	Manchester United	2–1
1958....	Bolton Wanderers	Manchester United	2–0
1959....	Nottingham Forest	Luton Town	2–1
1960....	Wolverhampton Wanderers	Blackburn Rovers	3–0
1961....	Tottenham Hotspur	Leicester City	2–0
1962....	Tottenham Hotspur	Burnley	3–1
1963....	Manchester United	Leicester City	3–1

* Won outright, but restored to the Association. † A special trophy was awarded for third consecutive win.

F.A. CHALLENGE CUP COMPETITION 1962 – 63

3rd Round	4th Round	5th Round	6th Round	Semi-Final	Final

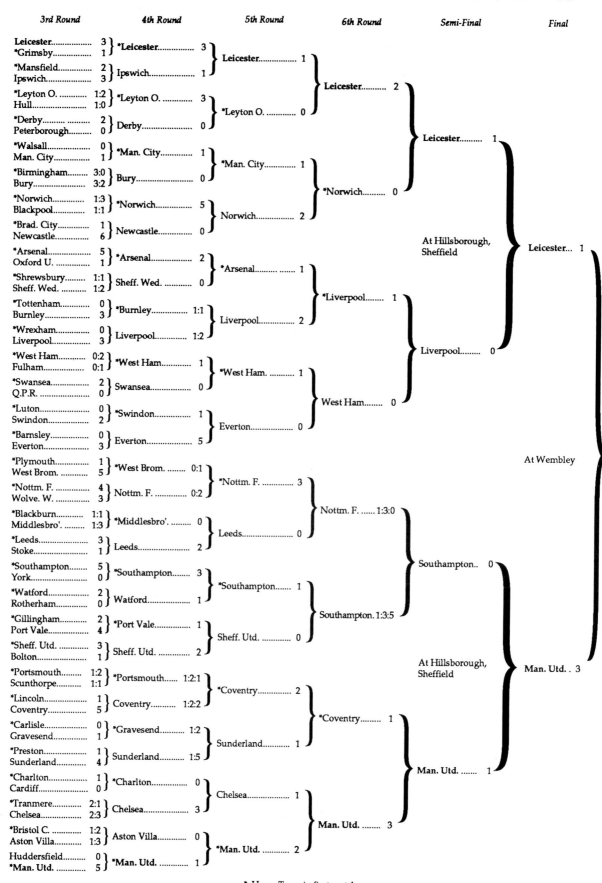

Leicester.................. 3
*Grimsby.................. 1 } *Leicester.................. 3
*Mansfield.................. 2
Ipswich.................. 3 } Ipswich.................. 1 } Leicester.................. 1
*Leyton O. 1:2
Hull.................. 1:0 } *Leyton O. 3
*Derby.......... 2
Peterborough.......... 0 } Derby.................. 0 } *Leyton O. .... 0 } Leicester.......... 2
*Walsall.................. 0
Man. City.................. 1 } *Man. City.............. 1
*Birmingham.......... 3:0
Bury.................. 3:2 } Bury.............. 0 } *Man. City.............. 1 } Leicester.......... 1
*Norwich.................. 1:3
Blackpool.................. 1:1 } *Norwich.................. 5
*Brad. City............. 1
Newcastle.............. 6 } Newcastle.............. 0 } Norwich.................. 2 } *Norwich.......... 0
*Arsenal.................. 5
Oxford U. .... 1 } *Arsenal.................. 2
*Shrewsbury.......... 1:1
Sheff. Wed. .... 1:2 } Sheff. Wed. .... 0 } *Arsenal............. ...... 1 } Leicester........... 1
*Tottenham.............. 0
Burnley.................. 3 } *Burnley................. 1:1
*Wrexham.............. 0
Liverpool................. 3 } Liverpool............. 1:2 } Liverpool.............. 2 } *Liverpool........ 1
*West Ham............. 0:2
Fulham.................. 0:1 } *West Ham.............. 1
*Swansea................. 2
Q.P.R. .... 0 } Swansea................. 0 } *West Ham. .... 1 } Liverpool......... 0
*Luton..................... 0
Swindon.................. 2 } *Swindon.............. 1
*Barnsley................. 0
Everton.................. 3 } Everton.................. 5 } Everton.................... 0 } West Ham........ 0

At Hillsborough, Sheffield

*Plymouth.............. 1
West Brom. .... 5 } *West Brom. 0:1
*Nottm. F. 4
Wolve. W. .... 3 } Nottm. F. .... 0:2 } *Nottm. F. 3
*Blackburn............. 1:1
Middlesbro'. .... 1:3 } *Middlesbro'. 0
*Leeds..................... 3
Stoke...................... 1 } Leeds...................... 2 } Leeds.................... 0 } Nottm. F. 1:3:0
*Southampton........ 5
York...................... 0 } *Southampton........ 3
*Watford................. 2
Rotherham.............. 0 } Watford.................. 1 } *Southampton........ 1 } Southampton.. 0
*Gillingham............. 2
Port Vale.............. 4 } *Port Vale................ 1
*Sheff. Utd. 3
Bolton...................... 1 } Sheff. Utd. .... 2 } Sheff. Utd. .... 0 } Southampton. 1:3:5
*Portsmouth.............. 1:2
Scunthorpe........... 1:1 } *Portsmouth...... 1:2:1
*Lincoln................. 1
Coventry................. 5 } Coventry............. 1:2:2 } *Coventry.............. 2 } *Coventry......... 1
*Carlisle.................. 0
Gravesend.............. 1 } *Gravesend............ 1:2
*Preston................... 1
Sunderland............. 4 } Sunderland............ 1:5 } Sunderland............ 1 } Man. Utd. 1

At Wembley

*Charlton............... 1
Cardiff..................... 0 } *Charlton............... 0
*Tranmere............. 2:1
Chelsea................. 2:3 } Chelsea............. 3 } Chelsea.................. 1 } Man. Utd. 3
*Bristol C. 1:2
Aston Villa............ 1:3 } Aston Villa............ 0
Huddersfield.......... 0
*Man. Utd. .... 5 } *Man. Utd. .... 1 } *Man. Utd. .... 2 } Man. Utd. 3

At Hillsborough, Sheffield

Leicester... 1

Man. Utd. . 3

* Home Team in first match.

58

United – v – City

In 1966/67 Alex Stepney was one of the newcomers to the team when United finished top position in the First Division, four points clear of Nottingham Forest. If you were to eavesdrop on pub conversations in the Manchester area at the close of the 1967/68 season two principal topics would be overheard. The title race between rivals City and United, plus the Reds' progress in the European Cup – both memorable moments in the Old Trafford story.

On the domestic front, the Blues and the Reds fought vigorously to outdo each other. Clearly, the Mercer-Allison combination at Maine Road was working well for Manchester City. Early in the season, United had defeated the Blues 2-1 thanks to a couple of Bobby Charlton goals, but on March 27th 1968 the Maine Road team were the victors in a 3-1 result.

The close of the season saw both clubs level at the last match. What a cliff hanger! City did well to secure a 4-3 away win at Newcastle, while the Reds lost 2-1 at home to Sunderland. The crowd of almost 63,000 was stunned as they walked away from Old Trafford knowing how the Final League position for 1967/68 would look:

	P.	W.	D.	L.	F.	A.	PTS.
1. Man. City	42	26	6	10	86	43	58
2. Man. Utd.	42	24	8	10	89	55	56

Europe 1967/8: the road to the Final

On the road to the Final, United beat Hibernians of Malta 4-0 (aggregate), before moving on to defeat the Yugoslavian team FK Sarajevo 2-1 (aggregate). In the quarter final games against Górnik Zabrze of Poland, tough soccer matches resulted in an overall 2-1 victory, giving United access to the European Cup semi-final.

The initial stage of the clash of the Titans saw the first leg played on April 24th at Old Trafford. The home team defeated Real Madrid 1-0 thanks to a George Best goal. The arena for the second confrontation was Bernabeu Stadium, Madrid where a crowd of 125,000 awaited the start of the 2nd leg of the semi-final. United were without Law who was experiencing trouble with a knee

injury, and so Sadler took his place. The dependable and reliable Bill Foulkes, now in his mid 30s, assumed the rôle of centre half.

The first 45 minutes of this historic tussle saw the English club trailing 3-1. But who can ever forget the last quarter of an hour in this thriller? Suddenly Sadler headed in United's second goal, following a free kick from Crerand. The atmosphere was electric as the minutes ticked by, and then a dynamic run by George Best was followed by a pass to Bill Foulkes who had dashed up from defence and now scored that all-important goal. At 90 minutes, both teams had three goals under their belts, but United won 4-3 on aggregate. They returned home victoriously with the 2000 fans who had followed them to Spain. As the stage was set for the European Cup Final against Benfica, United were 7-4 on to win the Cup outright, while Benfica were 11-8 against.

The '68 European Cup Final

Date – May 29th 1968. The opponents – Benfica. The venue – Wembley Stadium. The team – Stepney, Brennan, Dunne, Crerand, Foulkes, Stiles, Best, Kidd, Charlton, Sadler, Aston. Denis Law was recuperating after a cartilage operation.

Perhaps the most crucial game in United's history was about to start. The Portuguese club had a tremendous amount of pace and flair provided by stars such as Eusebio, but the first half of the game proved unspectacular. The last 45 minutes were quite different as the crowd shouted for victory. Bobby Charlton found the back of the net with a header, following a Tony Dunne cross, but then Graca provided an equaliser 10 minutes from the end. Could United snatch a goal?

Suddenly disaster loomed up as Eusebio lived up to all expectations and blasted a driving shot which Alex Stepney prevented from entering the goal. And so to extra time.

Matt Busby's encouragement during the break lifted his team who entered the second gruelling period of the battle. Seven minutes into this half, Best converted a pass from Kidd into a goal, swiftly followed by a Kidd header which foxed the Portuguese keeper. Bobby Charlton hammered home another goal. Victory to the Reds, 4-1.

Matt Busby was delighted – his dreams had been realised as United received the coveted European Cup in May 1968. The next month, this great man was made a Knight of the British Empire and became Sir Matt Busby.

The club was rewarded by an upsurge in numbers attending games, with the one millionth

European Cup Winners. United receive a tumultuous reception at Manchester Town Hall in 1968. They had beaten Benfica 4–1, with goals supplied by Charlton (2), Best and Kidd.

spectator to see United at Old Trafford in 1967/8, arriving at the City -v- United Match early 1968. For League games, the Reds were showing a post-war record average crowd of 55,353, and seats varied in price. At the "Derby" game between the two Manchester rivals, reserved seats were 10 shillings or 7 shillings and sixpence, while unreserved seats sold for 6 shillings. Bearing in mind that one shilling was 5 new pence, a useful comparison can be made of prices in the 1990s and those of some 20 years ago!

Sir Matt leaves

Chat to any United supporter about the most important event of 1969 and he will probably say the resignation of Sir Matt Busby following 24 years as manager at Old Trafford. This football genius assumed the mantle of general manager after his dynamic career was disrupted by the Munich air crash, from which he valiantly fought back to regain full health.

His accomplishments? A complete book would have to be dedicated to these if one were to give them justice. Some examples would be the League title of 1956/7, the rebuilding of United after Munich, plus managing a team which won the FA Cup in 1963. The culmination of his career must be the Wembley defeat of Benfica which brought Sir Matt's dreams to fruition when he saw the European Cup carried away by his beloved club.

A hard act to follow, Sir Matt was succeeded by Wilf McGuiness who occupied the manager's chair until 1970 when the great man stepped in again as manager until 1971. This allowed the club to take time in selecting a successor to McGuiness, with Don Revie and Jack Stein tipped as favourites in certain quarters.

Sir Matt was of course a United director, and then President of the club, and had been made a Freeman of Manchester in 1967.

United -v- City Again

In spite of the discussions surrounding the resignation of Matt Busby there was still time to savour the atmosphere leading up to the League Cup clash between United and City in December 1969. The Reds had already participated in the semi-final of the FA Cup that year, but their fans were still smarting from the League game against the Blues on November 15th when United were defeated 4-0. In the first Leg of the League Cup semi-final on December 3rd 1969, Colin Bell put City ahead after receiving a ball from Lee. Bobby Charlton scored United's only goal in the 2-1 victory for City.

At the semi-final second Leg match, a crowd of over 63,000 attended the Old Trafford clash on December 17th when Edwards and Law each contributed to a 2-2 draw, United losing 3-4 on aggregate.

The club was now carrying on with improvement plans for the ground, the previous five years having seen United spend £1 million on development schemes. In April 1971, work commenced on a new £400,000 stand. The building of a modern cantilever at the score-board end was started less than five years after the completion of the cantilever along the Trafford Park side of the stadium.

O'Farrell and Docherty

Having left a successful Leicester club in June 1971, Frank O'Farrell acquired several players during his 12 months as manager at Old Trafford. These included Martin Buchan, Ted MacDougall, and Ian Storey-Moore, while Welsh international Wyn Davies was signed from Manchester City for £60,000.

"The Doc"

The 1971/2 season saw United finish eighth in Division One, with the next couple of years providing food for thought as several people departed from Old Trafford, such as Gowling and Burns. New faces included manager Tommy Docherty who succeeded Frank O'Farrell in December 1972. A former Scottish International "The Doc" remained with the club until 1977 and saw the Reds through a difficult period. In 1973/4 for instance the club finished 21st in Division One, were relegated to Division Two for one season, and re-emerged in 1975/6 when they were a respectable third in the First Division.

Few of us will ever forget that all important relegation game at the close of the 1973/4 season when the Blues and the Reds faced each other. Mental arithmetic had indicated that one point could keep United clear of relegation if Everton beat Southampton and Norwich defeated Birmingham.

Exit Charlton

With hearts in their mouths, the fans of the Reds could never believe that an unfortunate piece of action would harm them so much. In the last 10 minutes one of Denis Law's tricky back heel goals gave City a 1-0 victory (Remember he had joined the Blues in 1973). One sympathises with the former United star, since this meant Division Two for his old club!

Moving back to other changes in personnel, Bobby Charlton departed in 1974 after some 20 years with United. January of the same year witnessed George Best playing his last game for the club, while the loyal player Tony Dunne moved to Bolton Wanderers in 1973.

Bobby Charlton's testimonial match was an occasion to be remembered, with just over 60,000 people paying tribute to the "Gentleman of Soccer" on September 18th 1972.

This modest man bowed out gracefully, still on top and with innumerable awards to his credit. He had won medals for the FA Cup, League Championship, World Cup and European Cup. Awarded an OBE in 1969, this legend in his own lifetime was voted Footballer of the Year and European Player of the Year.

Hill and Coppell

Tommy Docherty's team now featured players like Gordon Hill and Steve Coppell on the wings. They provided interesting moments for younger fans who hitherto had not experienced a soccer match with wingers. The 4-2-4 formation provided impressive performances from Hill and Coppell, the former scoring on 51 occasions with Steve Coppell supplying 70 goals. Tommy Docherty paid £60,000 to Tranmere Rovers for Steve who played nearly 400 games for the Reds before a knee injury forced him to quit the game. An intelligent young man with a university degree, Coppell displays tact and *savoir faire* when talking to the media and players.

His personality and experience have assured him of a career as a respected soccer club manager. He took Crystal Palace into 1991 as their manager for the seventh year, guided the club from Division Two to the one above, and saw them play in the 1990 FA Cup Final.

Hands in the air signify that the ball has not entered the net during this December 1971 confrontation between Stoke City and United. The final result was 1-1 with a Denis Law goal putting United on the score sheet. The two sides met again for United's last game in the 1971/2 season when a 3-0 victory for the Manchester club was provided by Best, Charlton and Storey-Moore. United finished eighth in Division One, while Stoke were seventeenth.

Martin Buchan holds aloft the Second Division Championship Cup in 1975, the Reds having obtained 61 points, while second place went to Aston Villa. In addition to receiving a medal for his part in this championship, Buchan also acquired another for being on a winning side in the F.A. Cup, plus two F.A. Cup Runners-up medals.

1976 FA Cup Final -v- Southampton

United had beaten Oxford, Peterborough, Leicester, Wolves and Derby before reaching Wembley on May 1st, 1976.

From the outset, United displayed clever, exciting football often involving a succession of passes between half a dozen players. The Manchester team almost scored when Hill tried for goal only to be kept off the score sheet by a superb save from Turner.

Gradually, Southampton entered the game more, throwing the United attackers off side three times in 5 minutes, while Osgood and Channon were becoming forces to be reckoned with. In the 83rd minute the decisive goal gave an unexpected score of 1-0 to Southampton who received the Cup and medals from the Queen. One bit of consolation for the United fans was that their team had provided some entertaining soccer throughout the 1975/6 season, losing only 10 matches in almost 50 League and Cup games. Perhaps this was why the United fans far outnumbered the Southampton supporters at the 1976 FA Cup Final, even though ticket touts were asking astronomical prices for tickets.

1977 FA Cup Final -v- Liverpool

Many of us can call to mind the confrontation between Liverpool and United, concluding in a 2-1 victory for the Manchester club. The Reds had reached Wembley with wins against Walsall, Q.P.R., Southampton, Aston Villa and Leeds.

Liverpool had everything to play for as they looked to the elusive 'Treble'. The Merseysiders were already League Champions and would be playing in the European Cup Final a few days after the Wembley game.

An uneventful first half of the FA Cup Final produced no goals at all, but Tommy Docherty must have given an inspirational talk to his team at the interval. The second half commenced with a superb pass from Jimmy Greenhoff to Stuart Pearson who drove a low volley past goalkeeper Clemence.

The Mancunian fans were ecstatic, but hardly had the cheering subsided when two minutes later Jimmy Case supplied the equaliser. The Liverpool contingent roared their approval, but in just under three minutes a Macari-Greenhoff move saw the Reds notch up another goal.

Liverpool substituted Callaghan for Johnson, and United still remained ahead, the 90 minute whistle heralding a superb 2-1 victory for United.

The United team comprised Stepney; Nicholl; Albiston; McIlroy; Buchan; B. Greenhoff; Coppell; J. Greenhoff; Pearson; Macari; Hill (McCreery).

So Liverpool would have to try for the 'Treble' on another occasion, and the club doubtless hoped that a rampant Manchester United would not stand in their way again.

New managers – and Wembley again

Dave Sexton succeeded Tommy Docherty as manager in 1977, the new man having taken Chelsea to the FA Cup Final and to the European Cup Winners' Final. He acquired a number of new players including Joe Jordan and Gordon McQueen from Leeds United, while Ray Wilkins was purchased from Chelsea for a fee of £825,000 in August 1979.

1978/9 was United's centenary season with the fans enjoying their team playing in the FA Cup Final for the third time in four years. Quite an impressive record. The route to Wembley was full of memorable games against Chelsea, Fulham, Colchester and Tottenham, and of course the semi-final involving old rivals Liverpool.

On March 31st the Manchester team met the Merseysiders at Maine Road when a crowd of 52,000 witnessed a nail biting 2-2 draw, United's goals courtesy of Jordan and B. Greenhoff. The replay took place on April 4th at Everton's ground where a single goal by J. Greenhoff assured United of a place at Wembley.

A highlight of the Final was surely the 2-0 lead which Arsenal held on to until just five minutes before the final whistle. The 100,000 crowd assumed the London club would walk away with the Cup, but then the old United flair and experience paid off. Superb goals by McQueen and Sammy McIlroy in the closing minutes produced a 2-2 scoreline.

Extra time seemed to be the order of the day when suddenly Alan Sunderland converted a Graham Rix cross into a goal. Final score – Arsenal 3, United 2. Even though United lost, how many can forget the last 10 minutes of this match on May 12th 1979? The exciting end to this Final must surely place it in the history books alongside the 1953 "Stanley Matthews Final". (This man virtually won the game for Blackpool after Bolton were leading 3-1, with only 20 minutes to go. However, a brilliant run by Matthews led to a Mortenson goal, who then shot the equaliser from a free kick. In the last 30 seconds a fine Matthews dribble allowed Perry to score from a superb centre.)

F.A. CHALLENGE CUP COMPETITION 1978 – 79

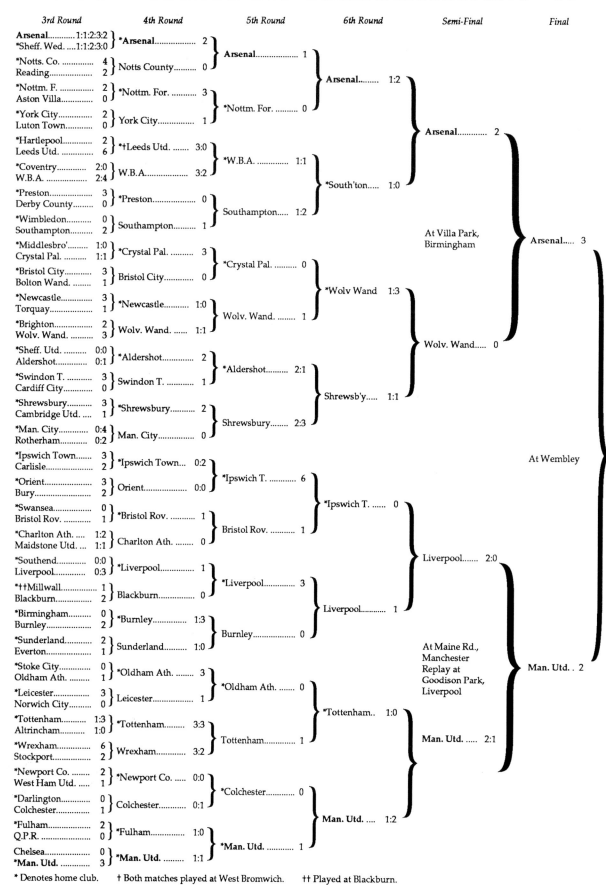

3rd Round	4th Round	5th Round	6th Round	Semi-Final	Final

Arsenal............1:1:2:3:2
*Sheff. Wed. ....1:1:2:3:0 } *Arsenal................. 2

*Notts. Co. 4
Reading.................. 2 } Notts County.......... 0

Arsenal................... 1

*Nottm. F. 2
Aston Villa............. 0 } *Nottm. For. 3

Arsenal........ 1:2

*York City.............. 2
Luton Town........... 0 } York City............... 1

*Nottm. For. 0

*Hartlepool............ 2
Leeds Utd. .... 6 } *†Leeds Utd. 3:0

Arsenal............. 2

*Coventry............ 2:0
W.B.A. .... 2:4 } W.B.A. 3:2

*W.B.A. 1:1

*Preston................. 3
Derby County........ 0 } *Preston.................. 0

*South'ton..... 1:0

*Wimbledon........... 0
Southampton.......... 2 } Southampton.......... 1

Southampton..... 1:2

*Middlesbro'. 1:0
Crystal Pal. .... 1:1 } *Crystal Pal. 3

At Villa Park,
Birmingham

Arsenal..... 2

*Bristol City........... 3
Bolton Wand. .... 1 } Bristol City............. 0

*Crystal Pal. 0

*Newcastle............. 3
Torquay.................. 1 } *Newcastle........... 1:0

*Wolv Wand   1:3

*Brighton................ 2
Wolv. Wand. .... 3 } Wolv. Wand. 1:1

Wolv. Wand. 1

*Sheff. Utd. 0:0
Aldershot............... 0:1 } *Aldershot.............. 2

Wolv. Wand..... 0

*Swindon T. 3
Cardiff City............. 0 } Swindon T. 1

*Aldershot.......... 2:1

*Shrewsbury.......... 3
Cambridge Utd. .... 1 } *Shrewsbury........... 2

Shrewsb'y..... 1:1

*Man. City........... 0:4
Rotherham............ 0:2 } Man. City............... 0

Shrewsbury........ 2:3

*Ipswich Town....... 3
Carlisle.................. 2 } *Ipswich Town... 0:2

Arsenal..... 3

*Orient.................... 3
Bury....................... 2 } Orient.................. 0:0

*Ipswich T. 6

*Swansea............... 0
Bristol Rov. .... 1 } *Bristol Rov. 1

*Ipswich T. 0

*Charlton Ath. 1:2
Maidstone Utd. ... 1:1 } Charlton Ath. 0

Bristol Rov. 1

*Southend............ 0:0
Liverpool............. 0:3 } *Liverpool.............. 1

At Wembley

*††Millwall............... 1
Blackburn................ 2 } Blackburn................ 0

*Liverpool............. 3

*Birmingham.......... 0
Burnley.................. 2 } *Burnley.............. 1:3

Liverpool............. 1

Liverpool....... 2:0

*Sunderland........... 2
Everton.................. 1 } Sunderland.......... 1:0

Burnley.................. 0

*Stoke City........... 0
Oldham Ath. .... 1 } *Oldham Ath. 3

*Leicester............. 3
Norwich City......... 0 } Leicester................. 1

*Oldham Ath. 0

*Tottenham.......... 1:3
Altrincham........... 1:0 } *Tottenham......... 3:3

*Tottenham.. 1:0

At Maine Rd.,
Manchester
Replay at
Goodison Park,
Liverpool

Man. Utd. . 2

*Wrexham.............. 6
Stockport................ 2 } Wrexham............. 3:2

Tottenham............. 1

Man. Utd. 2:1

*Newport Co. 2
West Ham Utd. ..... 1 } *Newport Co. 0:0

*Darlington............. 0
Colchester.............. 1 } Colchester............. 0:1

*Colchester............. 0

Man. Utd. 1:2

*Fulham.................. 2
Q.P.R. .... 0 } *Fulham............... 1:0

Man. Utd. 1

Chelsea.................. 0
*Man. Utd. .... 3 } *Man. Utd. 1:1

* Denotes home club.   † Both matches played at West Bromwich.   †† Played at Blackburn.

The stylish '80s

Ron Atkinson

April 1980 witnessed the departure of Dave Sexton from Old Trafford, even though the last seven games had resulted in victories for the Reds. Pundits deemed it necessary to develop a more attacking side, and with this in mind a new manager was sought.

Many a conversation in Manchester pubs in Spring 1980 revolved around the new appointment. Would it be Laurie McMenemy, Brian Clough or perhaps Bobby Robson? The successor to Dave Sexton was in fact Ron Atkinson, a former Oxford United player who went on to manage a couple of Southern League clubs before assuming a similar rôle at Cambridge United. He took them to the Fourth Division Championship and pointed them towards the top of the Second Division.

Moving from West Bromwich Albion to Old Trafford, Ron Atkinson was accompanied by some of his non-playing staff, together with Remi Moses and Bryan Robson.

Bryan Robson

Ask any United fan to cite one of the most important signings in the last decade, and you will probably be told, "Bryan Robson". A record British sum of £1.5 million was paid for the English international in October 1981 when he left West Bromwich Albion.

No book on United would be complete without outlining Bryan's illustrious career. His first game for the Reds was a somewhat dreary match against neighbours Manchester City enlivened only by Robson's flashes of inspiration. This player's dribbling, passing and shooting were faultless, and soon he became captain of both England and United, carrying on from Ray Wilkins at Old Trafford.

His contribution to United's success was phenomenal – leading the club to victory over Barcelona in the 1984 European Cup Winners'

Cup, and taking them to FA Cup Final victories. A tenacious, tough player, Bryan has been plagued by injury. For example, when he was with West Bromwich, he broke his Leg three times in one year!

Who can forget his contribution to soccer at World Cup level, with the 1982 Finals in Spain seeing Bryan score just half a minute after the kick off? In the same contest, in 1990, he was forced to retire early, returning home from the World Cup because of further injuries. This problem with his Achilles tendon has not deterred the man who in December 1990, played his first senior match for United since the FA Cup Final, where the Reds defeated Wimbledon 3-1.

Subsequent games during 1991 have seen Bryan in fine fettle, and on the international scene he turned out for the England 'B' side against Algiers in December 1990. In February 1991, he had nine complete League and cup games to his credit and represented England against the Cameroons in that month.

The close of the 1990/91 season saw Bryan tantalising opposition defences, as this player of high perception provided some superb examples of football skills.

The Early '80s

United were third in Division One at the close of the 1981/2 season. The following year saw Dutch International Arnold Muhren moving to Old Trafford from Ipswich Town. The early 1980s were important for United. They agreed an important sponsorship deal with Sharp Electronis and, in 1982/3. the Reds enjoyed their first Milk Cup Final; unfortunately, they lost 2-1 to Liverpool after extra time.

A decade ago United performed well in the League, FA Cup and in the League Cup. The Reds played in front of 1,198,529 spectators this season at Old Trafford – the highest attendance figures in the country.

The FA Cup 1982/83

There were record gate receipts at Old Trafford when over 58,000 fans paid £123,363 to watch the Reds beat Everton in the FA Cup Match.

Looking back to the 1983 Cup Final when Brighton held United to a 2-2 draw after extra time, perhaps the most dramatic moments were the goals from Stapleton and Williams, together with the plucky save by Gary Bailey. He snatched the ball from an approaching Robinson's feet in the last minute, thus making sure of a replay.

The team was the same in both games:

Bailey; Duxbury; Albiston; Wilkins; Moran; McQueen; Robson; Muhren; Stapleton; Whiteside; Davies.

Date	Round	Opponents	Result
Jan.8th	3	West Ham.	W. 2-0
Jan.29th	4	Luton Town	W. 2-0
Feb.19th	5	Derby County	W. 1-0
Mar.12th	6	Everton	W. 1-0
Apr.16th	Semi-final	Arsenal	W. 2-1
May 21st	Final	Brighton	D. 2-2 (A.E.T.)
May 26th	Final:Replay	Brighton	W. 4-0
A. E. T. =after extra time			

A crowd of 92,000 turned up to enjoy the second confrontation between United and Brighton when Robson scored from an Albiston pass. A couple of minutes later, Norman Whiteside provided the next goal for the Reds. Just before half time, the dynamic Robson put United three goals ahead, while the second half goal followed from a foul on Robson – Muhren scoring from the penalty spot. Manchester United 4, Brighton 0 was a fair result.

In August 1983, the Martin Buchan Testimonial match was held, the player moving to Oldham within a week of this tribute to him. Sadly, Steve Coppell also departed in 1982/3 owing to a serious knee injury, but as we have seen earlier, he then assumed duties as manager at Crystal Palace.

Jesper Olsen (left) was born in Denmark, playing for a Danish club before moving to the Dutch side, Ajax. The slightly built player joined United's ranks in July 1984, staying there 5 years before transferring to the French club, Bordeaux.

71

Action from the 1986-87 season, when United finished 11th in Division One. This is a scene from the Norwich City game on November 15th, 1986 when a 0-0 score was the result.

In 1987-88 United lost only 8 League games, and amassed a magnificent total of 81 points. One of the teams who defeated the Reds was Norwich City, pictured here on March 5th, 1988 when they secured a 1–0 victory.

The Milk Cup 82/83

During 1982/3, the Reds performed well in the Milk Cup, defeating Bournemouth, Bradford, Southampton and Nottingham before embarking on the semi-final against Arsenal.

Both Legs at this stage of the competition resulted in a 6-3 victory for United on aggregate, with the Final going into extra time. Eventually Liverpool beat United 2-1 at Wembley with Whiteside finding the consolation goal. He also secured himself a place in the annals of football history, as the youngest scorer in a League Cup Final.

First Division 1982/83								
Position	Team	P	W	D	L	F	A	Pts
1st	Liverpool	42	24	10	8	87	37	82
2nd	Watford	42	22	5	15	74	57	71
3rd	Manchester Utd	42	19	13	8	56	38	70

Hughes arrives – Wilkins goes

Early encounters in the 1983/84 season were very satisfying for supporters and players, since between 27th August and 29th October 1983, the Reds lost only two of their eleven games. However, January 1984 brought a shock 2-0 defeat by third Division Bournemouth in the FA Cup, while Oxford pushed United out of the Milk Cup competition in a 2-1 victory on December 19th, following a 1-1 draw twelve days earlier.

Mark Hughes now entered the United story. His first match saw him come on as a substitute in a 1983 Milk Cup game, with his full League début taking place in March 1984 against Leicester. Needless to say, Mark provided one of the goals in a 2-0 victory.

Born in Wales in 1963, he played for his country on many occasions, and between 1983 and 1986 he scored 47 goals for United.

Sadly, United did not manage to bring home the European Cup Winners' Cup, having reached the semi-final stages when Juventus beat the Manchester club 2-3 on aggregate in 1984.

In May 1984, Ray Wilkins left the Reds to play for AC Milan while during the close season, Gordon Strachan, Jesper Olsen and Alan Brazil were signed. It was about this time that further extensions to the cantilever roof were undertaken, and Bobby Charlton became a member of the Board of Directors.

The Everton Matches of '84/'85

Who can forget the numerous clashes with the Merseyside Club. Do you remember these?

Date	Match	Result
27th October	League game	Everton won 5-0
30th October	Milk Cup	Everton won 1-2
2nd March	League game	Draw 1-1
18th May	FA Cup Final	United won 1-0 (A.E.T.)

Meanwhile, the top of the 1984/5 First Division table looked like this at the close of the season:

First Division 1984/85								
Position	Team	P	W	D	L	F	A	Pts
1st	Everton	42	28	6	8	88	43	90
2nd	Liverpool	42	22	11	9	78	35	77
3rd	Tottenham	42	23	8	11	78	51	77
4th	Manchester Utd.	42	22	10	10	77	47	76

Actually, the FA Cup Final against Everton was a bit of an anti-climax, but one incident will stick in the mind for some time to come. This occurred after a tackle by Kevin Moran on Everton's Peter Reid (now manager at Manchester City), which led to Moran being the first player ever to be sent off in an FA Cup Final.

The Reds struggled on valiantly with 10 men, the final whistle signalling a score of 0-0, and this necessitated extra time. As the game progressed, Whiteside suddenly pounced on a pass from Hughes and United found the chance they had been waiting for – the Mancunians had won 1-0, and this with only 10 players!

Injuries: Atkinson's Departure

The 1985/86 season began with a club record of 10 consecutive First Division victories, but injuries led to United eventually finishing fourth in the League. Mark Hughes had signed for Barcelona at the end of the '85/'86 season, and his former club was now beset by injuries. Robson nursed a dislocated shoulder, while Gary Bailey was receiving treatment for knee problems.

Alex Ferguson assumed managerial responsibilities following Ron Atkinson's departure in November 1986, the new man having proved himself as Aberdeen's successful manager. Ferguson's career encompassed a number of clubs, including Rangers, St. Johnstone and Dunfermline. Alex introduced several changes at Old Trafford, moving Frank Stapleton from the team so that Norman Whiteside could move up front again. Rumour has it that the new boss told young players to have their hair cut, and he introduced more vigorous training. Alex Ferguson was convinced that increased fitness would reduce tiredness which can cause muscle damage. This of course, was of particular relevance to Bryan Robson, who in 1986 had made only 21 League appearances because of his shoulder dislocation and a hamstring injury.

Finishing 11th in Division One during 1986-87, United were knocked out of the League Cup by Southampton (4-1). One highlight in the FA Cup Competition brought rivals City and United together on January 3rd 1986. A Norman Whiteside goal provided the 1-0 victory for the Reds, but in the next round, United lost to Coventry with the same score.

Who was playing for the Reds around this time? The team for the City – v – United Cup tie was a typical line up:

Turner; Sivebaek; C. Gibson; Garton; Whiteside; Moran; Duxbury; Strachan; Stapleton; Davenport; Olsen.

The Return of Hughes

Some fans would have viewed United's second place in the 1987/88 Division One table as compensation for the defeat by Oxford United who knocked the Reds out of the League Cup in the quarter final stages. United had collected a superb total of 81 points but were still in second place of the League table, just behind Liverpool.

This was a time of comings and goings with Gary Bailey's knee injury ending his playing career at Old Trafford. He returned to South Africa to resume the University studies he had left in order to join United, and was replaced by 'keeper Gary Walsh. Another person to depart was Frank Stapleton (to Ajax), while new arrivals included Brian McClair and Viv Anderson, the first of these completing the 1987/88 season with a magnificent total of 31 League and Cup goals.

Talk to any Stretford-ender about this era and he will remind you that the dexterous Mark Hughes was reunited with the club in June 1988. This talented Welshman, rated as one of the world's best strikers, had of course spent 1983-86 with the Reds before moving to Barcelona. Scoring four goals in Gary Bailey's testimonial match in May 1987, Hughes had clearly impressed manager Alex Ferguson. Following a short spell with Bayern Munich, Mark signed for United in June 1988, for a reputed £1.5 million. "Worth every penny", was the comment by fans who were treated to dazzling displays by a forward line which included Brian McClair and Hughes.

During the 1987/88 season, United had reached the fifth round of the FA Cup only to be defeated 2-1 by Arsenal in February 1988. Later that year, Jim Leighton joined Old Trafford from Aberdeen. In spite of an impressive career with this club, and although playing just under 100 games for the Reds in 2 seasons, Jim was left out of the 1990 FA Cup Final replay, with Les Sealey assuming goalkeeper duties. In March 1991, Leighton joined Arsenal on loan until the end of the season.

The 1988/89 Season

A number of injury problems, coupled with a certain amount of bad luck contributed to United's finishing 11th in the Barclay's League (Division One). In this rather uneventful period of United's history, the club was defeated by Nottingham Forest in the sixth Round of the FA Cup (1-0) while Wimbledon eliminated the Manchester team from the Littlewood's Cup in November 1988.

Some familiar faces were missing from the team sheet this season with Paul McGrath moving to Aston Villa, Gordon Strachan crossing the Pennines to play for Leeds, and Norman Whiteside joining Everton's ranks. New personnel at Old Trafford included Neil Webb who was acquired from Nottingham Forest for £1.5 million, while Michael Phelan was bought from Norwich City. Again, Danny Wallace and Paul Ince moved to Manchester from Southampton and West Ham respectively, with Garry Pallister travelling down from Middlesborough. The combined total outlay for these players was in the region of £7m.

Take-over Talks

Two moments to remember (or forget) in 1989/90 were the discussions about possible takeovers at the club and *that* game against Manchester City. Following intense media coverage, the would-be buyer pulled out of the deal and normal routine was resumed at the club, the whole business soon forgotten. But can the fans ever forget that 5-1 defeat by Manchester City on September 23rd 1989? Perhaps one ought to add that the return match in February 1990 ended in a 1-1 draw.

The 1990 Final

United were embarking on what turned out to be a fascinating and exciting run up to the FA Cup Final. Do you remember those nail-biting replays and periods of extra time?Details of the earlier rounds make interesting reading:

DATE	ROUND	OPPONENTS	RESULT	SCORERS
Jan.7th '90	3	Nottingham Forest	W. 1-0	Robins
Jan.28th '90	4	Hereford United	W. 1-0	Blackmore
Feb.18th '90	5	Newcastle United	W. 3-2	Robins; Wallace; McClair
Mar.11th '90	6	Sheffield United	W. 1-0	McClair

Now, on to those dramatic matches played in April and May 1990. In the semi-final against Oldham at Maine Road on April 8th, the score remained 3-3 after extra time, with contributions by Robson, Webb, and Wallace. A memorable match, particularly since United were ahead on two occasions. The "Latics" displayed a confident air when they met their First Division neighbours, Joe Royle's team already looking to the Second Division title.

The semi-final Saga

We can now look at the semi-final in some detail. The scoring opened with a fifth minute Barrett goal, causing consternation among United fans. Once again, Bryan Robson proved his worth, receiving a Neil Webb pass and converting it to a fine goal. Unfortunately Bryan was taken off twenty minutes from the end, and just after this Neil Webb's header gave the Reds a 2-1 lead.

The crowd of 44,000 looked on in amazement as Oldham's Marshall found the back of the net a couple of minutes later. When the final whistle went, the score read 2-2. Sixty seconds into extra time provided a Wallace goal, and in the second half of this period, Palmer made it level at 3-3.

Dejected United fans trudged home speculating about the semi-final replay three days later at Maine Road. Surely a First Division club of United's stature would trounce the Oldham side on April 11th? This was the rhetorical question asked by those of us who were present, as once again extra time was the order of the day. At the end of 90 minutes the score was 1-1 thanks to a McClair goal. In the extra period, Mark Robins' contribution made it a decisive 2-1 victory for the Reds.

The 1990 FA Cup Final -v- Crystal Palace

What a season to remember! Following the drawn out battles against Oldham with the extra time played, United were hoping for a clear cut match at Wembley. This was not to be, as the FA Cup Final against Crystal Palace produced six goals after extra time! Of course, Steve Coppell, the United 'Old Boy', was now manager at Palace and he obviously relished the thought of this Final against United.

Even with extra time, the score remained 3-3 with United's goals coming from Hughes (2) and Robson. Five days later, on May 17th, United turned out again, this time with Les Sealey in nets. The single goal of the match was scored by Lee Martin and United walked away with the FA Cup.

The team comprised:

Sealey; Martin; Ince; Bruce; Phelan; Pallister; Robson; Webb; McClair; Hughes; Wallace.

In Spring 1990, sixteen goals were scored in the FA Cup semi-final games and in the Final, while extra time was the order of the day at three of the four matches. In spite of a poor League performance, finishing 13th in 1990, and United's exit from the Littlewood's Cup in the Third Round, the fans will remember the year as the time when the Reds gained the FA Cup for the seventh time.

Robson's Come-Back

United followers were thrilled on December 22nd 1990 when Bryan Robson started his first senior game since the FA Cup Final. The captain was given a deep-lying rôle in the match against Wimbledon, preparing him for his impressive England come-back against the Cameroons in February 1991.

United still suffered from injury problems and at one stage, at the end of January, manager Ferguson was unable to play Robson, Pallister and Ince. This did not radically detract from the team's overall performance and by January 21st 1991, the Reds had experienced only one defeat in the previous 20 League and Cup games.

The Rumbelows Cup and the 1991 FA Cup

Supporters speculated on the possibility of the 1991 Division One championship, but unfortunately teams like Arsenal and Liverpool had too much of a lead. It was strange to realise that the last time United were League winners was as far back as 1967.

Putting the Division One title race on one side, hopes were pinned on the Rumbelows Cup and the FA Cup. Who recollects the memorable 3-2 victory of January 23rd when a Mark Hughes hat-trick ruined Southampton's chances in the Rumbelows League Cup quarter final replay at Old Trafford?

Hughes again

A short time after this game, Third Division Bolton faced the mighty United in the fourth round of the FA Cup, and again 27 year old Hughes proved his worth. In the 79th minute, the tireless striker volleyed in a ball from a Lee Sharpe centre, scoring the only goal in the match.

Fame for Ferguson

Alex Ferguson will not forget February 1991 when he was presented with Barclay's Manager of the Month Award, and again when his squad encoun-

tered Leeds in the first Leg of the Rumbelows Cup semi-final at Old Trafford. The clubs had experienced two League draws with each other earlier in the season, and the semi-final resulted in a 2-1 victory for the Manchester club. Lee Sharpe scored the first goal in the 67th minute, while McClair's chip produced another ten minutes before the end of the match which was played on February 10th.

Alex Ferguson's players faced a crucial period at the end of that month. Important games included the FA Cup Fifth Round at Norwich, while a week or so later it was time to take on Leeds in the second Leg of the Rumbelows League Cup semi-final.

Norwich Voodoo

There seemed to be a voodoo surrounding clashes with Norwich. Since Ferguson had been manager at Old Trafford, his team had not once returned home as victors from the East Anglian club.

Little changed at the Carrow Road meeting on February 18th. The fifth Round of the FA Cup resulted in a 2-1 defeat for the Reds whose only goal came from McClair in the 37th minute.

Jolted by this defeat, the players concentrated on the Leeds game, visiting Elland Road with a goal advantage, at a time when 19 year old winger, Lee Sharpe was given a new five-year contract by United. Those of us who crossed the Pennines to experience the Second Leg of the Rumbelows League Cup semi-final were hoping for a win. We also wondered how 34 year old Gordon Strachan would perform. The one time United player now acted as Captain of the Yorkshire team.

True to form, the Reds won 1-0, the aggregate score being 3-1, with Lee Sharpe netting the only goal of the game in the 89th minute. The match of February 24th must surely be remembered not only for this late goal, but also for Les Sealey's valiant efforts to keep Leeds out of the game with his superb saves and lightning-fast reflexes.

The "Double"

United's name went into the history books yet again in March 1991 when Mark Hughes was presented with the Players' Player of the Year award, while Lee Sharpe received the Young Player Trophy from the Professional Footballer's Association. This was the first time a club had won the "double", and never before had a player won the senior award on two occasions.

Alex Ferguson will remember in March 1991

Mark Hughes feels the full blow of a Whitlow tackle during the semi-final first leg of the Rumblelows Cup against Leeds in February 1991. Manchester United won 2–1, in a game where rivals from across the Pennines battled it out for a trip to Wembley in the Final.

when a 3-0 win over Norwich provided the first victory against the Canaries since he took over as manager. Perhaps this could be seen as compensation for the two defeats by the East Anglian club in the previous season, and also for the FA Cup disappointment at Norwich.

Sunday April 21st 1991 was a sad day for the United followers, their team losing 1-0 to Sheffield Wednesday in the Rumbelows Cup Final. Ironically, the Yorkshire club had Ron Atkinson as their manager, and one can imagine what was going through the mind of the former Old Trafford boss as he left the stadium.

It was a 39th minute Sheridan goal which gave the Second Division club their victory, and with United experiencing some bad luck in the second half, the one goal difference remained until the final whistle.

Those of us who were among the 80,000 crowd at Wembley will never forget Sealey's accidental clash with Paul Williams. It placed a question mark over the United man's fitness for the forthcoming games in the European Cup Winner's Cup.

City and United

Rivals City and United faced each other for their 114th League confrontation on May 14th 1991, the Reds winning 1-0 thanks to a controversial goal. City manager Peter Reid insisted that the decider was a Colin Hendry own goal while Alex Ferguson retorted that it came from a Ryan Giggs shot. Suffice it to say that newspapers attributed the goal to Hendry. Consequently City were positioned fifth in Division One on May 5th, while United occupied sixth place.

Many of us remember only too well the League game against Crystal Palace on May 11th, just four days before the European Cup Winners' Cup Final in Rotterdam. In the domestic game, Pallister limped off before half time in a match where Ferguson left out six of his "stars" with the European fixture uppermost in his mind.

At the close of the 1990/91 season United finished sixth in the First Division, just one place behind rivals City:

POSITION	CLUB	POINTS
1	Arsenal	83
2	Liverpool	76
3	Crystal Palace	69
4	Leeds	64
5	Manchester City	62
6	Manchester United	58

European Soccer

Spring 1991 was dominated by United's European soccer fixtures. The European Cup Winners' Cup quarter final against Montpellier had its first Leg at Old Trafford on March 6th, when a 55 second goal from Brian McClair produced a feeling of euphoria on the terraces. The excitement lasted only until the eighth minute when a Lee Martin own goal made the final score 1-1.

Disconsolate supporters made their way home wondering what would transpire on March 19th when the return match against the French team took place. When the match was played, it looked as though the first half would end in a 0-0 score. However, during the four minutes of injury time, Blackmore blasted a 40-yard free kick which squirmed past 'keeper Claude Barrabe. A couple of minutes after the break, Phelan was tripped by a Montpellier player, allowing Steve Bruce to wrap up a 2-0 win for United with his ninth penalty of the season.

The Reds had won 3-1 on aggregate and were now in the last four of the European Cup Winners' Cup. The Manchester club took on Legia Warsaw while Barcelona and Juventus confronted one another. As we all hoped, United defeated the Polish side 3-1 in the first Leg. In the next meeting on April 24th, a scoreline of 1-1 meant that United won 4-2 on aggregate.

This was a well-deserved result considering that this match was played during a hectic period for the Reds, just 3 days after the Rumbelows Cup Final against Sheffield Wednesday.

The Lee Sharpe goal in the 1-1 game against Legia Warsaw evoked memories of Bobby Charlton's efforts which led to Benfica's downfall in 1968, when United were the first English club to acquire the European Cup.

At 19 years of age, Lee Sharpe had not even been born in 1968. In 1991, he helped notch up another achievement in the club's history. His cracking 29th minute shot into the roof of the goal was so similar to that of Charlton's in '68 – Bobby had sent the ball screaming into the net from the edge of the penalty area to make it a 4-1 victory over Benfica.

Lee Sharpe is following in the great tradition of such soccer maestros as Charlton, Best and Law.

And so the scene was set for the European Cup Winners' Cup in Rotterdam on May 15th. The Spanish giants, Barcelona, had already displayed their strength when Johan Cruyff's team lost only 1-0 with 10 men at Juventus, for a 3-2 win on aggregate.

Final of the European Cup Winners' Cup

The competition had certainly provided variety for the United faithful, who witnessed a fascinating run up to the Final. There was the match against Wrexham who finished the season at the foot of the Football League, while the climax involved the May 15th encounter with Barcelona, newly crowned champions of Spain.

The game was the most important match for an English club in six years. Twenty years before, of course, United became the first English side to win the European Cup, playing in blue, while Portuguese opponents Benfica wore in white in order to avoid a clash of colours.

In the 1991 game, United had white shirts and Barcelona turned out in blue. For Alex Ferguson it was the second time he had tasted success in this competition, having taken Aberdeen to that memorable 1983 win over Real Madrid.

The Game

So now on to that match to remember, where after a five year absence from Europe, the Reds presented a superb display of stamina and skills.

It was a moment to relish for the outstanding Mark Hughes who demolished his former Spanish club with two goals as the final score read, Manchester United 2, Barcelona 1.

The media had suggested that the tough style of English soccer could unsettle the Barcelona squad and this certainly proved to be the case. The first ten minutes brought millions to the edge of their seats as the televised game was seen in over 100 countries. It was in this early stage that a through ball from Robson saw Lee Sharpe try for goal and again Brian McClair had a shot at goal which whistled over the bar.

The rest of the first half was a quiet time for goalkeeper Les Sealey who was wearing a bandage on his injured knee. However, the second half proved more entertaining for the 25,000 United followers who had travelled to the Rotterdam stadium. Hughes was fouled by Alexanco in the 67th minute, and Robson sent across his free kick to the far post. Steve Bruce soared above the Spanish 'keeper to head goalward, with Mark Hughes pushing it over the line from a yard away.

The supporters were jubilant as Mark now seemed determined to remind Barcelona of what their former striker could really accomplish.

Escaping all the Spanish team's off side traps, Hughes then deceived the 'keeper and fired a low right foot shot inside the far post. The Welshman's revenge was complete. Would United win?

In the last anxious 10 minutes, Ronald Koeman pulled one back for Barcelona. With just five minutes to go, Hughes looked as though he might achieve his hat trick, evading one defender only to be upended by Nando a couple of yards from the penalty area, this resulting in the red card for the Spaniard.

He was the second player in the 1990/91 season's competition to be given his marching orders while tackling Mark Hughes. Remember Montpellier's Baills' dismissal at Old Trafford in the quarter final tie?

Tense moments now in the closing minutes as a Landrup shot was masterfully cleared off the line by Blackmore.

Suddenly it was all over! Alex Ferguson's name was entered in the history books as the first British manager to win the Cup Winner's Cup twice. The 2-1 victory guaranteed United a place in Europe the following season, along with Arsenal in the European Cup and Liverpool in the UEFA Cup.

With United rejoining Europe's élite it is an appropriate place to end this look at the club's story. The Reds had dominated Continental soccer for the first time since Sir Matt Busby's magnificent side clinched the European Cup in 1968.

The team had thrilled a world-wide audience with a bristling performance which resulted in the 2-1 victory over Barcelona.

A far cry indeed from those early days in 1878 when the Newton Heath club turned out on some spare ground in front of a handful of spectators.

THE ROAD TO THE FINAL

MANCHESTER UNITED

FIRST ROUND
Manchester Utd 2 (Blackmore, Webb) **Pecsi Munkas 0.**
Pecsi Munkas 0 Manchester Utd 1 (McClair).
Man Utd won 3-0 on agg.

SECOND ROUND
Man. Utd 3 (McClair, Bruce pen, Pallister), **Wrexham 0.**
Wrexham 0, Man. Utd 2 (Robins, Bruce)
Man. Utd. won 5-0 on agg.

QUARTER FINAL
Man.Utd. 1 (McClair) **Montpellier 1.**
Montpellier 0 Man.Utd. 2 (Blackmore, Bruce).
Man.Utd. won 3-1 on agg.

SEMI-FINAL
Legia Warsaw 1 Man.Utd 3 (McClair, Hughes, Bruce).
Man.Utd 1 Legia 1 (Sharpe).
Man.Utd. won 4-2 on agg.

BARCELONA

FIRST ROUND
Trabzonspor 1 Barcelona 0.
Barcelona 7 Trabzonspor 2 (Bequiristain, Amor, Koeman 3, Stoichkov 2).
Barcelona won 7-3 on agg.

SECOND ROUND
Fram Reykjavik 1 Barcelona 2 (Salinas, Stoichkov).
Barcelona 3 (Eusebio, Bequiristain, Pinilla) **Fram 0.**
Barcelona won 5-1 on agg.

QUARTER-FINAL
Dynamo Kiev 2 Barcelona 3 (Bakero, Urbano, Stoichkov)
Barcelona 1 (Amor) **Dynamo 1.**
Barcelona won 4-3 on agg.

SEMI-FINAL
Barcelona 3 (Stoichkov 2, Goicoechea) **Juventus 1.**
Juventus 1 Barcelona 0.
Barcelona won 3-2 on agg.

United's Achievements

FOOTBALL LEAGUE

Division One Champions: 1907/8; 1910/11; 1951/52; 1955/56; 1956/57; 1964/65; 1966/67
Runners Up: 1946/47; 1947/48; 1948/49; 1950/51; 1958/59; 1963/64; 1967/68; 1979/80; 1987/88
Division Two Champions: 1935/36; 1974/75
Runners Up: 1896/87; 1905/6; 1924/25; 1937/38

CUP VICTORIES

F.A. CUP Winners: 1909; 1948; 1963; 1977; 1983; 1985; 1990
Runners Up: 1957; 1958; 1976; 1979

LEAGUE CUP

1982/83
1990/91 – Runners Up

EUROPEAN COMPETITIONS

EUROPEAN CUP: 1956/57 (S.F.); 1957/58 (S.F.); 1956/57 (S.F.); 1967/68 (Winners); 1968/69 (S.F.)
EUROPEAN CUP WINNERS' CUP: 1963/64; 1977/78; 1983/84; 1990/91 (Winners)
EUROPEAN FAIRS CUP: 1964/65
UEFA CUP: 1976/77; 1980/81; 1982/83; 1984/85

Index